REVOLUTION

Emmanuel Macron was born in Amiens on 21 December 1977. After graduating from the *École nationale d'administration* in 2004, he worked in the Inspectorate General of Finances, and then became an investment banker at Rothschild & Co.

Macron was appointed Minister of Economy, Industry and Digital Affairs in François Hollande's government in 2014, and resigned in August 2016 to launch his *En Marche!* political party as part of his bid for the 2017 presidential election. He won the election on 7 May 2017 with 66 per cent of the vote, defeating the National Front's candidate, Marine Le Pen. His renamed party, *La République En Marche!*, won an outright majority at the legislative elections in June 2017.

EMMANUEL
MACRON
Revolution

Translated by Jonathan Goldberg
and Juliette Scott

SCRIBE
Melbourne • London

Scribe Publications
18–20 Edward St, Brunswick, Victoria 3056, Australia
2 John St, Clerkenwell, London, WC1N 2ES, United Kingdom

First published in French by XO Éditions as *Révolution* in 2016

First published in English by Scribe 2017

Printed and bound in United States of America by Lake Book Manufacturing

Scribe Publications is committed to the sustainable use of natural resources
and the use of paper products made responsibly from those resources.

9781925322712 (US paperback)
9781911344797 (UK hardback)
9781925548648 (e-book)

A CiP entry for this title is available from the the British Library.

scribepublications.com
scribepublications.com.au
scribepublications.co.uk

CONTENTS

Translators' notes

Translation is a journey over a sea from one shore to the other
… I cross the frontier of language with my booty of words,
ideas, images, and metaphors.
   –Amara Lakhous

Translating words is very different from casually reading them. The dictionary definition of any given word is often insufficient to convey its exact nuance in the context. The translator has to excavate the meaning and bring order to impressions, guesswork, and approximations and at the same time faithfully evoke the author's voice — his tone and style.

All translators work within two parameters: staying close to the source text, without being too literal, and going further afield without taking impermissible liberties. The clash between "literal translation" and "free translation" goes back many centuries — to Jerome, the patron saint of translators, or arguably earlier. In translating this book I often found myself groping for that fine line — the golden mean. Whenever I saw the light of day, it felt like a small victory on the path toward clarity and readability.

I was fortunate in my choice of collaborators. I could not have hoped for a more skillful and gifted co-translator than Juliette Scott, whose command of both English and French is quite remarkable. My other pillar of support was my wife, Andrea. She has a limited knowledge of French, but this was more than compensated for by her unusual ability to sculpt a draft translation into a final text of elegance. Her TLC—tender loving contribution—was one of the mainstays of this endeavor. Juliette, Andrea, and I dissected innumerable words and phrases, and tirelessly exchanged views until every word was acceptable to each of us. A truly synergetic endeavor.

To better understand those segments of the source text that I found cryptic or ambiguous, I turned to my friend and guru in all matters of French language, history, and culture—Jean Leclercq. His intellectual prowess, energy, and willingness to assist were an indispensable element of the collaborative enterprise.

Hélène Salomez also shared her considerable knowledge and insights across a range of subjects discussed in the book.

Jeremy Bernstein, my favorite journalist, gave generously of his time and expertise in reviewing the translation. The editing support of our publisher, Henry Rosenbloom, provided the cherry on the top.

Jonathan Goldberg, Los Angeles

Translation is always a fascinating task. In these few paragraphs I hope to share with you, dear reader, some of the reasons why that is so.

A text begins with its author. In being elected president of France and launching a political party with entirely new values and ways of working, Emmanuel Macron has proved to be an exceptional person, able to break with stale traditions. This book will give you information about who he is and what he hopes to achieve. It also conveys his great passion for bringing about positive change—a passion that has been missing from French politics for so long.

But the book does even more than that. Macron is a multi-layered person, and so are his words. You will find references to literature, history, and philosophy that twinkle like stars throughout, making this so much more than any kind of manifesto.

To translate such a work has been an honor. My co-translator and I have been faced with many decisions, at all times to ensure that the author's extraordinary voice can best be perceived by English-speaking readers. First, we were asked to address this version to a joint British, American, Canadian, Australian, and non-native readership. That has been challenging, to say the least. Perhaps it is also an international endeavour that you will appreciate as forming part of our collective global future. Second, we needed to convey a host of cultural references underlying the prose. With that in mind, you will find endnotes that are designed to provide further contextual background, but not to impinge on the flow—in other words, so that each reader can choose whether they need or want to find out more.

Whatever impetus led you to choose this book, and whatever the parallels with the situation in your country, I feel certain that Macron's words will resonate with you, as they have with so many of his supporters and the French electorate, and as they have with me during the time I have spent in the company of his ideas and convictions.

Juliette Scott, London

Prologue

To regain hope, we need to confront the reality of our world.

Some believe that our country is in decline, that the worst is yet to come, that our civilization is withering away. That only isolation or civil strife are on our horizon. That to protect ourselves from the great transformations taking place around the globe, we should go back in time and apply the recipes of the last century.

Others imagine that France can continue on its slow downward slide. That the game of political juggling—first the Left, then the Right—will allow us breathing space. The same faces and the same people who have been around for so long.

I am convinced that they are all wrong. It is their models, their recipes, that have simply failed. France as a whole has not failed. The country is vaguely aware of this—it senses it. And from there stems the "divorce" between the people and those who govern them.

I am convinced that our country has the strength, the resilience, and the desire to progress. Its history and its people make this possible.

We have entered a new era. Globalization, digitalization, mounting inequalities, the climate threat, geopolitical conflicts, terrorism, the disintegration of Europe, the democratic crisis in Western societies, the doubts pervading the heart of our society: these are symptoms of a world in immense upheaval.

We cannot respond to these great transformations with the same people, the same ideas, imagining that it will be possible to go back in time. Thinking that we can simply repair or adjust our organizations and our "model", as some like to call it, when no one—least of all ourselves—fundamentally wishes to take that as our inspiration any longer.

Nor can we expect the French people to make never-ending efforts by promising them a bogus way out of the crisis. This attitude, adopted time and again by our leaders over the past thirty years, has given rise to fatigue, incredulity, and even disgust.

Together, we must look the truth in the eye; debate great transformations that are underway; where we are going and the path to be taken; the time that such a journey will take. Because all this cannot be accomplished in one day.

The French people have a greater awareness of the new demands of our times than their leaders do. They are less conformist, less attached to those preconceived ideas that maintain the intellectual comfort zone of political life.

We must all forsake our habits — the state, political and business leaders, high-ranking civil servants, trade unions, and other interest groups.

This is our responsibility. It would be a mistake to shy away from it or to accommodate ourselves to the status quo.

We have become used to a world that we find disturbing, that deep down we do not wish to recognize or to confront head-on. So we grouse and grumble. In the midst of drama and despair, when fears take hold of us, we dwell on them. We want change, and yet we're not really committed to it.

If we wish to progress, make our country succeed, and build our prosperity for the twenty-first century in keeping with our history, we must act. Because the solution depends on us. Success does not depend on making a list of proposals that will not be implemented. The solution will not emerge from building dubious compromises. It will be created by a different approach that presupposes a profound democratic revolution. It will take time. It will depend on only one thing: our unity, our courage, and our common will.

It is this democratic revolution that I believe in. One through which, in France and in Europe, we will drive our own revolution rather than endure it.

It is this democratic revolution that I have ventured to outline in the pages that follow. They contain no program, nor any of the thousand-and-one proposals that make our political life look like a catalogue of failed hopes. Rather, they constitute a vision, a narrative, an aspiration.

It is the French people themselves who have the will, which is often ignored by their governments. I wish to serve that will. Because I have no other desire than to be of use to my country. That is why I decided to offer myself as a candidate for the presidential election of the Republic of France.

I am up to the demands of the office. I am aware of the grave times we live in. But no other choice appears to me to be more honorable, because it tallies with your own preferred choice to rebuild France, finding in that endeavor our energy and our pride in an enterprising and ambitious France.

I am resolutely convinced that the twenty-first century, which we are finally entering, is full of promises and changes in store that can bring us greater happiness.

This is what I offer you.

This will be our battle for France, and I know of none finer.

CHAPTER ONE

Who I am

As I embark on this adventure, I feel I have a duty to explain where I come from and what I believe in. Public life does not always allow for such explanations. I am now thirty-nine years old. Nothing predestined me for the position that I held as Minister of the Economy, nor for the political undertaking in which I am engaged today. I cannot really explain this trajectory. I see only the result, which, fundamentally, is always a work-in-progress, of a longstanding undertaking and an all-embracing taste for freedom, no doubt thanks to some good fortune.

I was born in December 1977 in Amiens, the capital of the Picardy region, into a family of hospital doctors. The family had recently entered the middle class — advancing, as one used to say, by toil and by talent. My grandparents were a teacher, a railroad worker, a social worker, and a civil engineer. They all came from modest backgrounds. The history of my family is that of the historical rise of

Republicanism in the French provinces between Hautes-Pyrenees and Picardy. Their advancement was achieved by dint of knowledge and, more precisely, for the last generation, through the medical profession. For my grandparents, this was a fast track, and they wanted to push their children in the same direction. That was how my parents, and then my brother and sister, became doctors. I am the only one not to have taken that path. This was on no account because of any aversion to medicine. In fact, I have always had a taste for the sciences.

But when it came to choosing the direction I wanted my life to take, I wanted my own world—an adventure of my own. For as far back as I can remember, I have always had that ambition: to make my own life choices. I had the good fortune to have parents who, while encouraging me to work, saw education as a training ground for freedom. They imposed nothing on me. They allowed me to fulfill my destiny.

So I chose my life as if, at each stage, everything had been laid out ahead of me. Things were not always easy, but at the same time they were not complicated. I had to work hard, but I had a taste for it. I suffered failures, sometimes painful ones, but I did not allow myself to be diverted after making my choices. It was in these years of training that I forged the conviction that nothing is more precious than the freedom to choose one's own future, the pursuit of a mission that one has set oneself, the realization of one's talent, whatever its nature. And talent is something that each of us possesses. This conviction subsequently determined my commitment to politics by making me sensitive to the injustices of a society based on the status quo, regimentation, classes, and social mistrust, where everything conspires to block one's personal fulfillment.

My grandmother taught me to work. From the age of five, when school was over, I spent long hours with her, learning grammar, history, geography … and reading. I spent entire days reading out loud to her: Molière and Racine, Georges Duhamel, an author somewhat forgotten, whom she loved, as well as Mauriac and Giono. My grandmother shared a taste for study with my parents, and my childhood was punctuated by their concerned expectation whenever I came home from the least important school examination.

I had that luxury, and it was priceless. My family was concerned for me, and at certain times nothing but that particular examination, that particular written page, counted for them. They expressed their care and concern with the words as sung by Léo Ferré, which have never ceased to move me: "Don't come home too late, and don't catch cold."

I learned those words in the cradle of my infancy, and they hold within them so many essential qualities: tenderness, trust, the desire to do the right thing. There are many who have not had the good fortune that I had. What people subsequently do with such fortune is, of course, another matter. But in that respect, too, I cannot think about the Republican school system today without remembering my family, whose values so profoundly matched its teachings, nor the teachers for whom it was an honor to overcome every limitation so that their pupils would achieve the best they could. Few countries can evoke such commitment, such love, and firmness of purpose, and we must ensure that future generations keep this flame alive.

And so it was that I spent my childhood immersed in books, a little removed from the world. It was a sedentary life in an average French town; a happy life of reading and writing. I lived largely through texts and words. Things took on greater significance when they were described, and were sometimes more real than reality itself. The secret, intimate course of literature transcended outward appearances, giving the world all its depth, of which we only get a fleeting glimpse in our daily routine. One is not removed from real life when one reads. My only voyages then were those of the mind. I became acquainted with nature, flowers, and trees through the words of writers, and was made even more aware by the spell that they created. I learned from Colette what a cat or a flower was, and from Giono about the chill wind that buffets Provence, and insights into human nature. Gide and Cocteau were my irreplaceable companions. I lived in happy seclusion in the bosom of my family—my parents, my brother, my sister, and my grandparents.

For my parents, education was essential. They always surrounded me with their boundless attention, and yet allowed me to make my own choices and to become independent.

For my grandmother, literature, philosophy, and great writers were more important than anything. Study had enabled her to change her life. She was born into a modest family in Bagnères-de-Bigorre, to a father who was a stationmaster and a mother who was a cleaning lady. She was the only child in the family to pursue study beyond middle school, whereas her sister and brother had to go straight out to work. Her mother could not read. Her father had trouble reading, and did not grasp nuances. She told me a story from her schooldays, when she was about twelve or thirteen and came home with a report saying "good at everything". Her father, reading this as "game for anything", understood it as a reproof of her loose morals, and slapped her. In her final year of school, she encountered a teacher of philosophy who saw her potential. He encouraged her to pursue literary studies by correspondence so that, a few years before the war, she received a diploma that qualified her to teach at Nevers. She took along her mother—today we would call her a "battered wife"—whom she would never leave until the end of her days.

My grandmother was a teacher. Having said that, let me detach the word from its humdrum connotation and give it the spark of her real passion. She lived her life with admirable devotion and patience. I remember reading letters written by her former students about their visits to her home. She had shown them the path by which knowledge leads to freedom. It was not, however, a life of hardship: after classes, they drank hot chocolate while listening to Chopin and discovering Giraudoux. My grandmother came from the same milieu as her students, primarily daughters of artisans or farmers from Picardy. She led them through the same stages of development that she herself had experienced, and opened for them the doors of knowledge, beauty, and perhaps of the infinite.

At that time, there was much prejudice to be overcome in the average family. Nothing discouraged my grandmother, perhaps because she was of an optimistic temperament, but above all because she knew, based on her personal experience, that what she wished to pass on was the best of what it means to be 'civilized', and that it was a matter of honor for the community not to deprive girls of such insights.

I was perhaps her last student. Today, she is no longer with us, and not a single day goes past without my thinking of her and searching for her presence. It is not that I am looking for the approval that she can no longer give me, but rather because I would like, in the work that awaits me, to show myself worthy of her teachings. I have often thought, in recent years, about veiled young Muslim women at school or university. It seems to me that she would have deplored these young girls being prevented by dogmatic pressures from gaining access to true knowledge, free and personal in its nature. But because she had devoted her life to the education of girls, and was able to measure to what extent such education could not be taken for granted, even in a country like ours, I believe that she would have deplored the fact that we could find nothing better than prohibition, confrontation, and all the hostility that runs so contrary to what we ought to be creating for our future. In this regard, nothing good can be achieved without love.

And I was lucky enough to have that love from her. I remember her face. Her voice. I still remember her reminiscences. Her freedom. Her exacting standards. Those early mornings when I would go into her bedroom, and she would recount anecdotes of war and of friendships. As a child, I would take up the thread of our conversation of the previous day, and I voyaged through her life as if returning to a novel. And the smell of the coffee that she would sometimes prepare in the middle of the night. And at seven in the morning, when the door of my bedroom was ajar before I had gone to her, when she would ask, with contrived concern, "Are you still asleep?" And all those other things that I would prefer to keep to myself and that unite us forever.

Conversations with my parents also revolved around books. It was from them that I discovered a different literature, more philosophical and contemporary. As well as discussions of a medical nature, in which hospital life, and developments in practices and research were the subjects of debate lasting for hours on end. Several years later, my brother, Laurent, who had become a cardiologist, and my sister, Estelle, a nephrologist, would take up the baton.

Fundamentally, from those years I learned to exert myself, and I learned how a desire for knowledge paves the way to freedom. Although, since then, I have discovered the pleasures of a hectic life and of responsibility, I have also experienced the joy of that sedentary life far removed from human hubbub. Our roots offer us protection. And, I believe, make us wise.

I had only two other interests: playing the piano and acting. My childhood passion for the piano has never left me.

I discovered theater during my teenage years. It was a revelation. For me, proclaiming on stage what my grandmother and I had read together so often, listening to other actors, creating a shared moment, making the audience laugh or cry, was inspiring.

It was at high school, through theater, that I met Brigitte. Love sneaked up on us unawares. Initially it was through a meeting of minds that then developed into an emotional closeness, and, after that, without resistance from either of us, a passion that endures to this day.

Every Friday, I would spend several hours writing a play with her. That carried on for months. When the play was completed, we decided to stage it together. We discussed everything. Writing became a pretext for seeing each other. And it came to me that it was as if we had always known each other.

A few years later, I had managed to create the life that I desired. We had become a couple, inseparable, despite the headwinds.

At the age of sixteen, I left my home region for Paris. The move to the capital is one that many young adults make in France. For me, it was a marvelous adventure. I went to live in places that existed only in novels. I followed the paths of characters in Flaubert and Hugo. The consuming ambition of Balzac's "young wolves" carried me away.

I loved those years spent on the Left Bank.

Every day provided new learning opportunities. But I have to admit that although I had been top of my class every year in Amiens, I no longer really distinguished myself. I discovered in the students around me exceptionally talented individuals, real mathematical geniuses, whereas I was much more the diligent student. I must also confess that in those first years in Paris I chose to enjoy life, and to live and to love, rather than to throw myself into competitive studies.

I had a single preoccupation and purpose: to live the life I had chosen with the woman I loved. I did everything I could to achieve this.

The doors of the *Ecole normale supérieure* remained closed to me, and I made a conscious decision to enroll in the philosophy program at Paris Nanterre University, and then, as luck would have it, was admitted to Sciences Po.

These were happy years, always stimulated by free study, discovery, and meeting people. I loved those places as I loved the people who had taught me so much. I was fortunate enough to make the acquaintance of the philosopher Paul Ricoeur, thanks to the kindness of my history professor, who was his patient biographer. It was a fortuitous meeting at a time when he was looking for someone to archive his documents.

I will never forget the first hours we spent together at Murs Blancs, his home, in Châtenay-Malabry. I listened to him. I was not daunted. This was due, I must confess, to my complete ignorance: Ricoeur did not make an impression on me, because I had not yet read his work. When night fell, we did not turn on the lights. We stayed and talked, building a rapport.

That night marked the start of a unique relationship, in which I worked on his texts, providing comments, and accompanied him to his readings. For more than two years, I learned from him and worked at his side. I was not qualified to fill that position, but his trust in me compelled me to grow as a person. I read and learned more every day, thanks to him. He conceived of his work as a continuous reading of great texts, he who so often described himself as a dwarf standing on the shoulders of giants. Olivier Mongin, François Dosse, Catherine Goldenstein, and Thérèse Duflot became friendly and vigilant presences during those years, which transformed me so profoundly.

At Ricoeur's side, I studied the previous century, and learned to think in historical terms. He taught me the seriousness with which certain subjects and certain tragic moments should be treated. He taught me how to think about life through texts. In a constant to-and-fro between theory and reality, Paul Ricoeur lived among texts, but with a desire to illuminate the course of the world, and to make sense of our daily existence. Never to allow facile emotions or what others say about us to get the better of us. Never to get entrenched in a theory that does not confront reality. It is in such a state of permanent but fruitful imbalance that thought can progress, and political transformation can take place.

We are what we learn to be at the side of our masters. This intellectual apprenticeship transformed me. That was Ricoeur, with his critical demands, his obsession with the real world, and his trust in others. I know that I was very fortunate indeed to have known him.

Over those years, I formed the conviction that what inspired me was not simply to study, to read, or to understand, but rather to act and seek to bring about concrete change. I therefore turned to law and economics. It was then that I chose to go into public service. Along with a few others, who became and have remained faithful friends, I prepared for the competitive examinations for admission to the National School of Administration.

I was accepted, and was immediately sent to do a year's internship in the civil service. That is where government employees begin their practical training and acquire initial experience.

I enjoyed that year of internship and learning. I have never supported dissolving the National School of Administration. What is wrong in our system is rather that the careers of high-ranking officials are too shielded by the status quo, whereas others have to move with the times.

And so I began my service to the state at the French embassy in Nigeria. During those six months, I had the good fortune to work with Jean-Marc Simon, a remarkable ambassador. Subsequently, I was appointed to work at the Prefecture of the *département* of Oise. That allowed me to discover a different facet of the state—the state at a grass-roots level, locally elected representatives, the civil service. Throughout all those months, I was filled with enthusiasm, and I forged solid friendships that still endure, first and foremost of which was with Michel Jau, the then prefect.

It was then that I met Henry Hermand, who was to become so important to me, and who has recently passed away. From the outset, our association was one of friendly kinship and a shared passion for political engagement. This exceptional man was not only a successful entrepreneur, but also a fellow traveler for decades in his commitment to progressive policies for France. It was he who introduced me to Michel Rocard.

In 2016, they both passed away within a few months of each other. Over the last fifteen years I continued to see them both regularly: in private moments, for personal and political discussions. Even beyond our differing ages, experience, and the posts we held, Michel Rocard and I were very different. He was more committed to party politics than I was, and had a desire to change them by any means. His intellectual rigor, his determination, and his friendship made a profound impression on me. He was the first person to inspire me with a concern for our world—whether in historically significant international affairs, or in the cause of climate change, for which he fought for thirty years, including more recently the protection of polar zones.

That period spanning my studies at the National School of Administration was an unexpected one. I didn't really have the vocation or any points of reference. My grades were therefore a happy surprise, which offered me choices. In my chosen role of finance auditor, I discovered a new world. It was, admittedly, a world of administration, but the novelty of it enthralled me. For four-and-a-half years I learned the rigors of auditing, and acquired a wealth of experience that can only be gained from fieldwork in a variety of locations—the close collaboration involved in public service, and the progress that comes from working shoulder-to-shoulder with colleagues.

I thus had the opportunity to crisscross the territory and to spend entire weeks between Troyes, Toulouse, Nancy, Saint-Laurent-du-Maroni in Guiana, and Rennes. There were moments of camaraderie in which I learned to analyze and unravel the multiple mechanisms of the state and its officials.

It was at this time that I became Deputy Rapporteur-General of the *Commission pour la libération de la croissance française* (Commission for the Liberation of French Growth), presided over by Jacques Attali. For six months, I had the good fortune to work at his side along with the forty members of the commission, a number of whom were to become my friends. The commission gave me the opportunity to meet outstanding women and men—intellectuals, government employees, and entrepreneurs who make France what it is—to learn from them, but also to become aware of a number of issues in which I have never since lost interest.

Following those years, I chose to quit the "Service", as it is called, and to go back to the private sector and the world of business.

I wanted to learn its grammar, to tackle international issues, at the same time knowing that one day I would go back to public life. Throughout those years, I maintained a continuing interest in politics—by contributing to the journal *Esprit*, by keeping company for a time with close associates of Jean-Pierre Chevènement, and then by joining, albeit temporarily, the Socialist Party, where I did not find my place, although it enabled me to explore the Pas-de-Calais region where, over time, my family and I built strong ties.

And so it was that I left the public sector to join the merchant bank Rothschild & Co. Everything there was new to me. For several months, I learned procedures and methods from the youngest as well as the more experienced. Then, under the guidance of the most well-versed, I delved deeper into this strange profession, which requires an ability to understand a business sector and its challenges, to advise business leaders in their strategic choices, and to provide them with support in executing them, surrounded by a pack of technical experts. Over the years, I discovered the considerable power of commerce, but above all I learned a lot about the world.

I neither share the enthusiasm of those who hold a life in business to be the ultimate horizon of our times, nor do I support the bitter criticism of those who regard money as a leper and the symbol of man's exploitation of man. Both those perspectives appear to me to be flawed by a childish romanticism that is irrelevant in our era.

I spent much time with outstanding colleagues. David de Rothschild, with much intelligence and grace, is adept at gathering such people to his side. They are highly talented, and their personalities would normally not allow them to work together. The banking profession does not simply involve the management of money. It is not simply a matter of lending or speculating. It is a consulting profession, in which value lies in people.

I regret nothing of the four years spent at the bank. This period has been held against me more than once because those unfamiliar with that universe have only a fanciful idea of what goes on there. I acquired a profession there. All political figures should have one. I encountered many business sectors in many countries, and this has served me well ever since. I mixed with decision-makers, which is always instructive. I earned my living there, without making a fortune that would exempt me from working.

In 2012, I made a principled choice to leave the bank and to return to public service. Two years prior to that, I decided to commit to politics and to prepare the program and the ideas of the reformist Left in economic matters, at the request of François Hollande. After being elected president of the Republic, Hollande made me a proposal to join the team at the Élysée. I worked with Hollande for two years as Deputy Secretary-General, handling matters relating to the Eurozone and the economy.

I will keep my counsel about those years, because privacy forms part of my conception of serving the state. Advice is a matter for those who receive it. I hope that I gave good advice, whether it was followed or not. Without doubt, my advice was not all good. I take full responsibility for that. And not everything was done well. I asked to be relieved of my duties two years later. I left my position in the government in July 2014.

I did not apply for a political post, or a managerial post in a large firm, or in the civil service, as is often the case. I preferred to work, as they say, on my own account, to take on new projects and to teach. I did not plan to go back into politics. An overzealous "ethics" commission more or less banned me from seeing the president of the Republic again. These excesses are laughable, so far are they from reality. I paid no attention to them. I was taking a different path. And then I was called back by the president to become Minister of the Economy, Industry and Digital Affairs.

The rest belongs more to the public domain. I tried to take action, and I received support. I spent hundreds of hours in parliament in order to promulgate a law that I deemed beneficial—a law to remove obstacles, give access, support economic activity, revitalize purchasing power, and create jobs.

I wanted to set out an ambitious industrial policy, based on innovation and investment. Our priority was to protect our long-weakened industrial sector with energy and passion, enabling spectacular recoveries to be made, as with PSA Peugeot-Citroën and Chantiers de l'Atlantique. I sought to initiate a policy of "clear-sighted voluntarism", to fight relentlessly for the benefit of our industries and our economic sovereignty, whether in problematic restructuring, as in the nuclear or oil and gas sectors, or to protect French steel. It is not that I have ever had illusions regarding the limited power of public intervention to remedy desperate situations. And I have had failures that I recognize with regret. By supporting investment, and by mobilizing our industrialists in order to provide concrete solutions and develop "French tech", I sought to prepare the industry of tomorrow. Because the winds of change are blowing over our country in this domain, too.

Then came a time of obstacles and disagreements.

After the Paris attacks in the autumn of 2015, I witnessed what seemed to me to be errors, and sometimes even serious political mistakes: the abandonment of a strategy that was indispensable in order to seize new economic opportunities in our country, the absence of a real desire for reform and a greater European ambition, and the choice of a sterile debate on the withdrawal of citizenship — a debate that divided the country without providing a response to events. When financial crisis and society's despair were feeding into extremism and violence, at a time when our neighbors were finding solutions to permanently reduce unemployment, the real state of emergency that needed to be declared was, in my view, one of an economic and social nature.

I did not hide these differences of opinion. As for my actions as minister, they were hindered by the cumulative effect of misjudgments, a lack of people with technical expertise to call on, and the personal hidden agendas of others. I decided to take a political initiative by launching the movement *En Marche!* on 6 April 2016, in Amiens, the city of my birth. Whatever difficulties we encountered, that initiative was never intended to be "anti", but "for". As Malraux said, "Anti does not exist." I am very much a man of the "for" camp. For trying to overcome political divisions, the negative consequences of which I had determined. For going the extra mile to reconstruct our country. For building something new. For picking up the thread of our history and the momentum of progress. For a better life for our children than that of our parents. For building upon the desire prevalent in French society to get involved again. For bringing to the fore fresh faces and new talents.

In the following months, it became obvious that I needed to quit the government. I had to be true to my perception of things, to the men and women who were following me, to my conception of our country.

I'd like to say a word here, and no more, to clear up the stories of betrayal that were told about me. Underlying them is, in my opinion, the moral crisis in contemporary politics. What is implied when those voices say that I should have mechanically obeyed the president, renounced my own ideas, and subsumed the execution of what I believed to be right to his own future? Simply because he had appointed me as a minister? What is implied is that the public good should take second place to an ostensible debt of gratitude. I was amazed to observe the naivety with which those who sought to bring me down were thereby admitting that for them politics essentially followed the law of the underworld: obedience in the hope of being personally compensated. I believe that what makes the French turn away from politics or take up extreme positions is their instinctive aversion to those customs.

I attribute the words of the president of the Republic regarding my indebtedness to him to an aberration. I know him to be too committed to the dignity of public office and to the founding values of Republican political life to have subscribed, even if only momentarily, to that destructive idea of mutual back-scratching as a way of fulfilling obligations. That is also the reason why, while maintaining my respect for him, I took leave of him with a heavy heart. He had given me the opportunity to serve my country, at his side, and then as a member of the government.

I owe my allegiance only to my country—not to a party, a position, or a person. I accepted the duties that I took up only because they allowed me to serve my country. I stated that at the outset, and I never deviated from my pledge. When the obstacles placed in my way, the absence of new ideas and new people, the terrible lack of imagination, and the general torpor showed me that useful work was no longer possible, I drew the necessary conclusions and resigned. My concept of official duties is neither one of promoting a career nor of waiting in line for promotion. It is one of a shared commitment, based on service. Nothing else counts for me, and certainly not the criticism or calumny of those whose loyalty is reserved not for their country but for a system in which they know exactly how to use every single benefit and monetary advantage for their personal gain. That's what things have come to.

Throughout those years, Brigitte shared my life. We were married in 2007. That was the official consecration of a love, initially clandestine, often concealed, and misunderstood by many before they came to accept it.

I was probably stubborn in struggling against the circumstances of our lives where everything conspired to keep us apart, and in objecting to the commonly accepted norms, by which we were condemned from the outset. But I have to say that her courage was what stood out. The generous and patient determination was hers, and hers alone.

At that time, she had three children and a husband. For my part, I was nothing more than a student. She did not love me for what I had, for my situation, for the comfort or security that I offered. She gave up all that for me. But she did it with a constant concern for her children. Not by ever imposing anything, but by gently helping others to understand that the inconceivable could become reality.

Only much later did I understand that her will to bring our lives together made our happiness attainable. It was thanks to Brigitte, I believe, that her children gradually understood and accepted our relationship. I hope we have succeeded in building another family—not a typical one, but one in which the forces that bind us are all the more indestructible.

I have always admired that commitment and that courage of hers.

Firstly, in her role as French and Latin teacher. She has never ceased to exercise, in her exacting but kindly way, the profession that she entered thirty years ago and that she loves above all. I have seen her spend so many hours with challenged adolescents. Because she has that caring compassion and understands their fault lines. Because behind the resolute liveliness there is a world of sensitivity accessible only to the fragile, where they can find themselves.

Later, as a mother, she showed the same loving determination. She has always been there for each of her children throughout their lives and their studies. She has always been present while giving a strong sense of what she expected of them. Not a day passes without Sébastien, Laurence, and Tiphaine calling her, seeing her, consulting her. She is their compass.

So it was that my life was progressively filled by her three children, their spouses, Christelle, Guillaume, and Antoine, and by our seven grandchildren, Emma, Thomas, Camille, Paul, Élise, Alice, and Aurèle. It is for them that we are fighting. I do not devote sufficient time to them, and in their eyes these are stolen years. This gives me a further incentive not to waste the years we have together. Our family is the bedrock of my life, my anchor. The history of our country has inculcated in us a tenacious will not to concede anything to conformity when our belief is strong and sincere.

CHAPTER TWO

What I believe

Here, in a few pages, I will sum up my life, at least that part which is relevant to a life in politics. I have sometimes had to explain my career path, which may be perceived by some as that of an ambitious man in a hurry. I don't see it that way. Even from an early age, I realized what I owed to others—not only to my parents, my grandparents, or my teachers, but to successive generations who left us with a love of liberty gained at a price of great hardship.

I acknowledge my debt to those who put their trust in me. But, first and foremost, I am indebted to our country. My awareness of these obligations spurs me on to action.

So, yes, in following that path, I decided not to pay any dues to a political system that has never really recognized me as one of its own. If I have defied the rules of political life, it is because I never really accepted them. I believe deeply in democracy, and in the vigor and vitality of a politician's relationship with the people. At the same time,

I want to rediscover the essential richness of direct contact with the French people, by listening to their anger, by taking into account their expectations, by addressing their intelligence. This is the choice I have made. My aspiration is to engage my compatriots directly and to invite them to become engaged in turn.

I do not believe that our country must submit to the elitist conformity which teaches us that a life-long career in politics is a precondition for aspiring to the highest positions. I am persuaded that maintaining true independence from the system, while at the same time being intimately familiar with how laws are made and the process of public decision-making, is a real strength. In any event, this is what spurs me on in the battle that I have launched.

Our situation today is neither acceptable nor sustainable. In the face of events, we take refuge in our sad passions: jealousy, defiance, dissension, petty-mindedness, and sometimes baseness. The culture that I inherited is, by contrast, one of great and joyful passions: for freedom, for Europe, for knowledge, and for universal values. All we must do is regain our zeal and recognize the accomplishments that such a culture can bring. My purpose in writing this book and in committing myself to action is to participate in the movement that we need and in which we will rediscover our soul.

When politicians write about themselves, and especially about what they want to accomplish, they are rarely believed. They have no cause to complain about this.

One cannot at the same time enjoy both the advantages of power and the admiration of the public. To be at the center of a group, to be waited on as in ancient times, to enjoy fame that is often not acquired by one's talents alone—all these are intoxicating but rather base little pleasures. They are also rather dangerous, because one can indulge in politics and disappear from public life thirty years later without ever having done anything worthwhile. But at the end of the day this doesn't add up to much. Because for me, only action and accomplishment count. Without them, political life lacks honor. It is this taste for action, for transformation, that many elected representatives carry within them and which motivates them in their daily lives. For this reason, it is wrong to make them the target of the collective resentment of the moment.

Politics is not, and never should be, a "regulated profession". Representative democracy offers in my eyes an entirely different quality, which is found in mayors and many elected local officials. Our country has 600,000 of them, two-thirds of whom are volunteers. They do not count their working hours, they are often the object of criticism, and they work for the common good. The same goes for many elected representatives and decision-makers who have worked for decades to support their families. They have taken risks, and at the same time have embraced political action out of a love of their country and public endeavor. It is essentially for this reason that I wanted to commit to politics—to proclaim our greatness and what I believe is now possible for our country.

To this end, we need to do whatever is required. Our country is beset with doubt, unemployment, and divisions of a material but also a moral nature. Over this desolate terrain blow gusts of disoriented opinion and self-interested declarations by politicians who make a living from this kind of unrest. I cannot resign myself to that. Does this mean that we have to wait for the nod of an individual, a politician, or an election, even a presidential one? I do not believe so, because I am a French democrat.

As a democrat, I believe that the people possess reserves of energy unsuspected even by those who claim to speak in their name.

As a French citizen, I believe that it is our destiny to revive the thread of our history that has seen us hold an unparalleled place in the family of nations for more than a thousand years. France is loved for its rank among the nations, for the voice that it carries, for its culture, its strength, its people, its language, its talents. France is true to itself, strong and proud, when it retains that rank. Our country is still capable of this. It simply needs to rebuild its strength. That is where we stand.

The work of politicians, especially at a state level, does not consist of telling the nation what to do or subjugating it. Their work consists of serving the nation. In order to serve it, after so many deadlocks and failed policies, we must place our trust in that firmness of purpose that, although currently hard to discern, still endures in the people's desire for what is good and just.

So it is not for the state to regulate, prohibit, and then

to monitor and sanction. The state should not pose as the guardian of a social body that is judged, arbitrarily, to be weak and incapable of achieving good on its own. On the contrary, the nation should be allowed to rediscover the creativity of its great history. Society should be allowed to take initiatives, to experiment, to find suitable solutions. General de Gaulle, like Pierre Mendès France, demonstrated better than anyone that politics must face reality. I subscribe to that.

Being in politics doesn't mean being dogmatic either. Nothing runs contrary to my conception of politics more than stubborn ideology. Our compatriots do not expect those in charge to conduct abstract political debates. They expect their leaders to give meaning to their lives and to develop practical and efficient solutions.

The venture cannot be taken for granted, in particular for the political class. Engaging in politics assumes going beyond thought patterns that are convenient and in some respects comfortable, but which offer nothing beneficial —by which I simply mean whatever may contribute to building a world that is more acceptable and more just.

The grand policies of the past, those that were beneficial to our country, were always inspired by this spirit. General de Gaulle, more than anyone else, had a sense of France's greatness. Nevertheless, he deliberately renounced the French empire, which as a child he had learned was an integral part of that greatness, because he understood that the future of the country lay in Europe. No one had a greater sense of justice than Pierre Mendès France. But in

1945 he turned himself into the apostle of budgetary rigor, even in opposition to de Gaulle, because he saw, beyond outward appearances, how laxity could bring about social misfortune.

I cannot resign myself to being confined within the divisions of another time. My desire to go beyond the conflict between the Left and the Right was misrepresented by the Left as neoliberal treason, while the Right depicted me as the hypocrite of the Left. I cannot accept seeing a desire for justice impeded by old patterns that leave no room for personal initiative, responsibility, and inventiveness. If by neoliberalism one means trusting people, I agree to be branded as a liberal. Because what I defend, on the other hand, should enable everyone to find in their country a life that fulfills their deepest hopes. If, on the other hand, being on the Left means believing that money does not bestow all rights, that the accumulation of capital is not the ultimate aspiration of one's personal life, that civil liberties must not be sacrificed on the altar of an absolute and unattainable security, that the poorest and weakest must be protected and must not suffer discrimination, then I gladly consent to be branded as a man of the Left.

Our current political life is organized around a longstanding division, which no longer allows us to meet global or national challenges. First, the Left and the Right are divided even on the very principle of subscribing to the idea of the Republic and the place of the Catholic Church. These divisions are focused on defending the interests of industrial capitalism, where the Left defends the workers and the Right the owners. Whereas today, in fact, the key questions of our age are employment, which has been profoundly disrupted by environmental and digital challenges; new inequalities; our relationship with the world and with Europe; and the protection of individual freedoms and an open society in a dangerous world. The Left and the Right are profoundly divided on each of those issues, and, consequently, they are impeded from taking action. They have not updated their thinking to meet the reality that surrounds us. The major parties are continuously in search of imperfect compromises so as to ignore these divisions and participate in the elections.

What is there in common between a conservative Left that defends the status quo, and favors the closing of borders and leaving the Eurozone, and a social-democrat reformist European Left? Almost nothing. This is exactly what has made the functioning of government so difficult over the past four years. This is what has led to some reforms being curtailed and others being relinquished. What is there in common between a Right that favors an introverted identity that has never actually existed, that accuses Europe of all evils, that favors a brutal social policy, and remains ambiguous in economic matters, and a Right that is European, neoliberal, and socially progressive? Hardly anything either, and this is what brought about its defeat in 2012. The same divisions are currently at work in the debate among those on the Right.

However, every five years each camp wants to restate the importance of party discipline, of joining forces as the only way to survive in the face of the specter of the National Front. Our Republic is ensnared in political machinations. The primaries were invented for that purpose: to designate a leader because the party no longer has any shared ideology, empathy, or respect for any single candidate. The primaries also serve to effectively dispense with a first round because people are so certain that the National Front candidate will get through to the second round that they cast tactical votes as early as the first round, whereas in the past they would have voted according to their beliefs in the first round and more tactically at the second stage. Our political parties are dying because they no longer confront reality, but they still strive to take control of the general election for their survival. This fatigue with democracy, and the disappointments that the new system brings about, feed into its weakening and the inexorable advance of extreme positions.

Since the trauma of 21 April 2002, nothing has changed. The political class and the media are a band of sleepwalkers who refuse to see what is coming their way. From time to time they express outrage, but without drawing the necessary conclusions. So we see the same faces and we hear the same speeches. They spout the same points, the same proposals, which are changed before being applied, only to be later debated anew with much media fanfare. I regard this form of communication as a sickness that has taken over from conscience, honesty, talent, and perseverance.

Alongside the sleepwalkers, going along like sheep, are

the cynics, who are unable to think outside the box—they, too, are legion. Those who know that changes must be made, but can't see how their interests might be served, and imagine that the National Front will allow them to access power more easily.

If we do not bring ourselves to our senses, within five or ten years, the National Front will accede to power. There is no longer any doubt about this. We cannot, after each terrorist attack or each election loss, call for national unity, ask the country to make sacrifices, and think that the political class for its part can continue its petty business as usual. That would be a moral misjudgment and a historic wrong. And our compatriots know this. It is not a question of attacking those who vote for the National Front. I have always considered that to be an error. I know too many French citizens who have voted that way, not out of conviction, but simply to protest against an established order that has forgotten them, or out of pique. We have to touch people's lives. Give them direction and vision, and fight this party that is manipulating their anger.

It is for this reason that I sought to establish a new political force that we named "*En Marche!*" Because the real division today is between the backward-looking conservatives who are offering the French people a return to the old order, and the progressive reformers who believe that the destiny of France is to embrace modernity. Not to sweep everything aside or to slavishly follow the way of the world, but to look it squarely in the face and win back our rightful place.

CHAPTER THREE

Who we are

The time has come to bring France into the twenty-first century. That is our challenge.

It wasn't until 1914 that we entered the twentieth century, and it happened with a bang. The year 2015 painfully ushered in the twenty-first century, and yet we still refuse to see the big picture. To embrace this new era, we must be able to reconcile what we are in our hearts with what we need to become.

Now, what is France and where have we come from? I have already said that from my earliest years I have retained the most intimate bond with my country: the bond that I established with the French language. The heart of what unites us is to be found there. In its words, sometimes hackneyed, sometimes rediscovered, is a language that transports all of our history and has brought us together since Francis I had the brilliant idea at Villers-Cotterêts of building the realm on the basis of language. During the

Classical Age, French lost its Rabelaisian truculence, and for a long period coexisted with numerous dialects from which it pilfered nuances. From Brittany to the Basque country, from Alsace to Provence and as far as Corsica, many remained attached to that diversity and to the richness of their regional tongues. Our language conveys our history.

This is what really makes us an open nation, because a language and the images and memories that it evokes are learned together. Whoever studies French and then speaks it becomes the custodian of our history and becomes French. To become French is not only a question of having identity papers. I have known foreigners who did not live in France and who became French by virtue of their love for the French people. To fail to give such love its due would make us remiss in our mission, and nothing would be worse. If we had to find any meaning in the expression, which I do not like, "French through and through", it would refer not only to those whose families have lived in Mayenne for ten generations, but also to someone who, whatever their origin and wherever they live, honors the French language. Nothing moves me more than the French spoken in Guiana, in the Caribbean, in the Pacific. It is there that we find the true French language of our ancestors, those forebears who had come from all corners of the world, who then settled all around the globe, and who continue to make us a great nation.

My first memory of France was that of driving across the country to reach our vacation destination in the Pyrenees: a dozen journeys that merge in my memory to become one, that of the great countryside that unfolds between Amiens and Bagnères. Then there came the almost unreal charms of the Poitevin marshes, the harsh light of the Bordeaux area described by the writer Mauriac, and the Landes forests of pine trees with that smell of turpentine which permeated everything. Finally, the Pyrenean mountain range appeared on the horizon, the end of the journey, a refuge in time, a place of joy.

I was then a child of the provinces, a word that I always preferred to "territories", which is used today. For me, having been born in Somme, Paris had all the promise of amazing experiences and magical places. The world of *Arsène Lupin*, of *The Count of Monte Cristo*, and of *Les Misérables* was all around me, and like all those who love to dream, I imagined my heroes appearing on almost every street corner.

For each of us, the life of our country is made up of such small odysseys. And those thousand French journeys weave the invisible map of a France that is both single and diverse, mysterious and transparent, loyal and rebellious. There is no feeling that I understand better than attachment to the land. Each of us has our place in France that we cling to, our lodestar. André Breton, who loved Paris so much, arrived one day by chance on the borders of the Lot area, and discovered Saint-Cirq-Lapopie. He exclaimed: "Now I have no further desire to be anywhere else." I never tire of contemplating the unwavering and yet elusive soul of France, where time has turned into space. It is a heritage that precedes our conscious memory, and the taste of a future that will remain true to the hopes of the past. A country made up of words, and of land, rock, and sea. That is France.

But France is more than this. It is also a state and even an endeavor. It is a liberating nation.

Our history has made us children of the state, and not of law, as in the United States, or of maritime trade, as in England. It is both a splendid heritage and a dangerous one.

The state formed the nation by conquering frontiers, by creating rules, by establishing equality before the law throughout the territory. It embodied the Republican enterprise in places where the right balance was difficult to find, as witnessed by the succession of our political regimes. When the continuity of our history needed to be assured after 1789, it was to the state that the French turned. The importance for us of familiar figures such as the minister, the prefect, the director, or the mayor stemmed from a need to be united, to serve the same cause, a varied, multi-faceted nation that was unable to define itself as easily as many others and yet that believed it was called to a great destiny. And it was also the state that, over the course of time, recognized the place of each person in our national history.

This explains why the French state is so intimately linked with the very soul of both individuals and groups.

The state took on the mission of emancipating the

Republic in a very concrete way. It did so by affirming individual liberties and developing education under the Third Republic through the social achievements of the Popular Front; and by revitalizing the country in 1945 and in 1958. The state was able to take action, overcoming many vicissitudes, because the vision was broad, and it generated support and allegiance. It was further reinforced because palpable and concrete progress was made by all. For many years, the French were like recluses in their villages. Their new-found mobility—a mobility made possible by public education, and by the development of a rail and road infrastructure—enabled the enterprise to take shape. The role of the state has always been, and still is, to ensure that barriers are removed, to provide increased access and mobility, offering everyone the means to make a living. New systems have developed, but the stakes are the same as ever. Telephone coverage—cell phones and landlines—a driving license, public transportation, ride-sharing and the coach, and access to the Internet are all as imperative as the completion of the road network was in the past.

That is where the danger lies, and we have to be careful to take its measure. To attain its objectives, the French state has developed, by general consent, a heavy and complicated machinery intended to consistently guarantee equality and safety, two values that we cherish. But when the enterprise weakens and the vision is no longer discernible, that machinery spins its wheels in the absence of momentum and becomes an obstruction and a burden for the whole nation. Hundreds of entities that should have disappeared still exist. Public officials perform useless tasks. Regulation overruns everything, because it is more convenient to promulgate a law or a decree than to give direction. In so doing, public employees find a *raison d'être*, and politicians find a pretext to justify their privileges. The regulation itself takes precedence over the reasons for its creation. The country serves the administration, rather than the administration existing for the good of the country. Bit by bit, reality recedes. The world of power builds imaginary constructions.

But none of this is inevitable, and it is a mistake to see the state, merely for dogmatic reasons, as an evil in and of itself. Instead, we must take a long-term, practical view of the state — its relationship to our history, and the services it does and can render. For some, the state should be able to do everything, including spending money that it does not have. For others, the state is the source of all evil, and the solution is to demolish it. In fact, neither of these views is valid. Because the Republic, our common enterprise, which brings us together, is woven around the state.

I fear that the fine word "Republic" has become a cliché, so much has it been brought into disrepute. It is used to dismiss what one does not like — intolerance, fanaticism, a disdain for liberty — without, for all that, saying what it actually embodies. Intellectuals seek to distinguish it from democracy in order to support or oppose it. Great minds, with faux naivety, ask themselves which monarchy threatens us to the point that we are now obliged to invoke the Republic. How should we make allowance for what has not always been praiseworthy in "the Republic"? The Republic is not only a declaration of rights. It is also the massacres of the Vendée, colonialism followed by the excesses of the colonial wars, censorship of books, and special courts, which existed until recent times.

What is good is not always Republican, and what is Republican is not always good. If this were not the case, we would have applauded the Republican courts that sentenced Captain Dreyfus until the belated trial exonerated him, and we would have retained penal colonies and the prohibition on women's right to vote that the Republicans went along with for decades, until General de Gaulle put an end to these practices. We would also have had to support the denial of women's right to abortion, which lasted until Valéry Giscard d'Estaing understood their distress; and maintaining the death penalty, until François Mitterrand abolished it. So what exactly are we talking about here?

The Republic that we love and which we must serve is that of our collective liberation: freedom from superstition, whether religious or political; freedom from social prejudices; freedom from all those forces that come together to enslave us without our always being aware of them. The Republic is our mission, a mission that is never completed but that always remains a goal to be accomplished.

A song as obviously familiar as *Le Chant du Départ*, so familiar that we hardly pay attention to the lyrics, says it very well: "All French people must live for the Republic." It speaks less of an obligation than a reality. For a long time, the French have lived for emancipation and liberty.

"Republicans are adults; slaves are children." The French know that they cannot live under tyranny—not the tyranny of power, nor that of outmoded organizations, prejudices, circles of influence, and pressure groups. To be Republican means not consenting to anything that is opposed to our values. It is the embodiment of our collective honor. In a letter written during wartime, General Diego Brosset, a Companion of the Liberation, wrote a short time before his death at the head of his division: "One cannot find rational reasons for acceptance."

Our France, Republican by its nature, has enemies. Republicans should never refrain from naming them. What these various enemies all have in common is that they are fantasists, and sometimes wicked fantasists—prudes, utopians, exalting the past. They believe that they own the truth about France. This is not only dangerous, but untrue. The only French truth is our collective effort to gain our freedom and be the best that we can; an effort that must project us into the future. The enemies of the Republic seek to enclose it within an arbitrary and static definition of what it is and what it should be. The Islamists wish to enslave it, and, as experience shows, offer only hardship and slavery. The National Front, inspired by an absurd nostalgia for something our country has never been, would make it betray its very soul. There are those who join the ranks of the extreme Right by adopting its precepts. There are the cynics who flee France or scorn it. This is a very long list—but, at the same time, there are not enough of them to hold us back.

And it is, in fact, this mission that France has carried with it for so many centuries, that gives it its place, its rank. That same mission has fostered France's historical and continued influence in the world. From the Renaissance through the Age of Enlightenment, by way of the American Revolution and up to the Universal Declaration of Human Rights and anti-totalitarianism, France has contributed to bringing light to the world so as to liberate it from the yoke of ignorance—from religions that would enslave it, and from violence that negates the individual. There is in the spirit of the French people an aspiration for the universal that is both a constant protest against injustice and submission, and a deep desire to tell others of their conception of the world, here and now, and for the benefit of all. The spirit of the Encyclopedists, led by Diderot, is probably the quintessential expression of that delirious ambition, an ambition that represents us. Nothing could be further from what we are than for us to withdraw into ourselves.

CHAPTER FOUR

The great transformation

There is a feeling of gloom in France about what has become of the country — that it is sliding into the unknown, has lost its identity and the control of its own destiny. Ever since I was old enough to listen to political debate, I kept hearing that our country was in the midst of a crisis. This sentiment is a symptom of the French malaise.

It is a result of the new order we are entering, which unsettles us and is perceived by many of our compatriots as a threat, an attack on who we are. While the march of civilization is a historical process of evolution — of material, social, cultural, and political progress — for them it is synonymous with decline, a loss of control, and heightened anxiety and insecurity. But does this mean that the way of the world can be diverted? I don't believe so. We can, however, make drastic changes once we understand the basic dynamics.

This new order is also characterized by a society whose

boundaries are no longer those of a single country, but of the world. It is predicated on a constant and omnipresent global flow of goods, money, and people.

It disrupts a configuration founded primarily on nation-states, which, at a time when most of these exchanges took place within individual countries, determined almost all aspects of our lives. Over the course of decades, principles of commerce and finance came to dominate our world. And states became bureaucracies that tried to resist or support that economic reality without being able to fully control it.

I grew up in regions that experienced the harmful consequences of these metamorphoses. Whether in Amiens or Bagnères, textile regions, tens of thousands of jobs were eliminated during my youth. This occurred because the factories and woolen mills became less competitive, and people could more cheaply purchase clothes elsewhere — at that time from the Maghreb, and later from Eastern Europe, then China, and now Vietnam. And today you need do nothing more than speak to farmers in the area of Lozère, for example, to fully grasp this aberration: a world that no longer offers them a livelihood, in which they are obliged to sell their livestock at a price considerably lower than thirty years ago, despite the fact that their overheads are constantly rising.

The flows of globalization continue to accelerate. They create an interdependence amongst nations, companies, and research hubs. This is not always negative. Close to two million French citizens work in foreign firms located in France, and several million of our compatriots make a living thanks to exports. Not far from Bagnères, which I mentioned earlier, the aviation sector is flourishing, thanks to globalization. Airbus and so many others have invested, conquered new markets, and achieved success. So it would be false to claim that by abandoning globalization we could attain a better life. In fact, it is an iniquitous lie, because such an exit would probably create even more victims.

These profound changes have put an end to gradual collective advances, assured over decades, and have ushered in a more rapidly changing economy with its radical and sudden technological developments. Our forebears grappled with war and poverty, and lived through more difficult times than our own, but they were sustained by the prospect of progress. The feeling of making progress gives us a positive view of the future and an inner conviction that if we work hard, life can soon be better for us, and will certainly be better for our children.

We have moved beyond the decades in which France reconstructed itself, when there was a profound belief that the economy could make up for lost time and provide an arena for great projects. Then, as now, there were painful situations, regions that suffered after losing factories at the whim of social change, but hope endured—people were optimistic about potential new career paths and continuing progress. Today, by contrast, the idea of a permanent crisis has solidly embedded itself in people's minds, and is accompanied by the fear that they and their families will almost inevitably lose their social positions. Hardly anyone now believes that growth will suffice to assure our future. And those who have this belief do not know how to attain it, or cling to the pipedreams of closed borders and a country of national workshops financed by miracles.

What is more, globalization has accelerated and intensified in recent years, thanks in particular to burgeoning international finance, which facilitated developments in trade and then took on a momentum of its own. This development has its positive side because it has enabled national economies to be financed more rapidly and under more favorable conditions. However, it has also had the effect of rewarding activities that do not create the slightest real value and whose only goal is speculative. The financial system as it is currently organized has fueled the greed of certain individuals. All this has led many of our compatriots to reject finance as an institution across the board. And yet, we need it. At the end of each year we borrow money on the financial markets to pay our public officials. If our businesses win new customers and take on staff, that is in large measure thanks to the financial system. In this regard, we have to be discriminating—by opposing finance for its own ends while encouraging finance that promotes investment.

In fact, since the crisis of 2008, we have collectively done the opposite. We have not reined in all the excesses, and, on the other hand, we have stepped up curbs on banks and insurance companies, despite the fact that they play a central role in the financing of economies worldwide. It is principally at European and global levels that such a battle needs to be conducted. It is not just an economic battle, but a political and moral one. The current situation gives a large number of our compatriots a feeling of profound injustice. Facile responses that would work only in France or would sanction only some of the people involved solve nothing. They pander to a negative outlook without offering anything meaningful. What we really need are international measures and a spirit of unity.

Finally, globalization has taken a new turn in these past fifteen years with the development of the Internet and the digital age. This is where new frontiers are opening up to us. New practices and new paradigms have completely changed not only the way in which we manage our affairs, but also our horizons. We are changing our habits. More and more, French people order their meals, do their shopping, make payments, book their train tickets, and rent their vehicles online. We are changing our manufacturing processes. Software and the Internet contribute to new forms of automation. This industry of the future is transforming our businesses, making certain manual tasks less arduous, and requires accelerated training for many workers. Three-dimensional printing enables small volumes to be manufactured where they are needed, and has led to a rethinking of logistic approaches that on occasion led to goods being produced at the opposite end of the world from their place of consumption.

Our occupations are changing. According to business forecasts, several dozen new occupations will come into existence in the next few years; others have already seen the light of day in the last decade: community managers, specialists in big-data handling ...

At the same time, however, entire facets of the economy are undergoing profound changes. Studies show that between 10 per cent and 40 per cent of jobs may be automated in the coming twenty years. In banking and insurance, one-third to a half of the skills that employees currently possess will no longer be needed five to ten years from now. Robots and algorithms will do the repetitive work of many employees faster, more reliably, and at a lower cost—and at any time of the day or night. Digitalization will profoundly shake up the organization of our society. On the one hand, many middle-class occupations, and especially those of salaried workers, will be threatened; on the other, there will be new opportunities for jobs requiring very low or very high levels of skill. This is a fundamental point, as until now our democracy has been based upon these very people—a middle class that is today living in a state of uncertainty for their own future and that of their children.

The professional world we have known for so many decades is being revolutionized. Companies will no longer be the workplace for people's entire lives under permanent contracts. Working hours will become independent from places of work: people may work at their company's premises, at their clients' offices, in co-working spaces, or from home. They will leave their company, business sector, and position more and more often. This transformation is inevitable.

The ways in which we carry out research and innovation are also being revolutionized. Borders between disciplines are becoming blurred. The convergence of genomics, nanoscience, connected devices, and big data make possible discoveries that were previously unimaginable. Data growth is exponential. In the last few years, we have produced more data than ever before. Medical treatment is benefiting from these innovations. Our knowledge is progressing in an unprecedented manner. However, at the same time, new moral stances are emerging. Groups are coming into existence to pursue radical projects—such as "transhumanism" and "enhanced humans"—that challenge the very essence of humankind.

This technological transformation will continue to have significant implications not only for manufacturing, but also for our society. We are only just beginning to develop artificial intelligence. Today, it enables us to increase productivity and to replace repetitive tasks, while bringing with it job losses. Very soon, it will compete with human intelligence, and this will have multiple social consequences. Clearly, we have to prepare for upheavals, the scope of which we cannot comprehend today.

And the authorities will have a decisive role to play, bearing in mind the ethical and social implications of these developments.

These are profound changes in our collective psyche. With the advent of the Internet, we can now all see everything that goes on, comment on everything, and compare ourselves with others all over the globe. This gives us a liberating feeling that anything is possible. It brings together individuals with shared interests. At the same time, it feeds neuroses, and exposes cruel social injustices and differences in standards of living. By showing the lifestyles of the richest to the poorest, it can even nurture frustration and indignation. The Internet disseminates pornographic images, the impact of which has not yet been fully addressed. It may also enable murderous groups to establish themselves and thrive, by capturing the visual imagination of potential recruits. The digital age is characterized by its ability to foster both the best of everything and the worst.

Digital technologies are not limited to an economic sector, but represent a complete transformation of economies, societies, and political systems. These new technologies open up opportunities for people, and at the same time promote segregation by creating cliques and closed groups. It is an acutely decentralized way of organizing society, where each person can play a role and take power. Society is being reshaped because every individual can find their place in the crowd. One can therefore clearly see the challenge of our current social order: it globalizes and at the same time individualizes. In this way, it undermines all the traditional ways of organizing society, and in particular the role of the state as an intermediary. The new social order runs through and transcends all aspects of the traditional state.

Besides this, our societies are undergoing a demographic sea change: ageing in developed countries, demographic transition in developing countries, and the increase in world population all constitute profound transformations that have started and will continue to turn our infrastructures and lives upside down.

At the same time, we now find ourselves in a society at risk. There have always been wars. They were in the natural order of things. But new global risks have materialized, with which we are now only too familiar.

Environmental risks are there for all to see. They have been manifested in tangible and brutal catastrophes such as Bhopal in India in 1984, Chernobyl in the USSR in 1986, and Fukushima in Japan in 2011. But they are also more insidious — the gradual disappearance of wildlife (populations of vertebrates, fish, birds, mammals, amphibians, and reptiles plummeted by 58 per cent between 1970 and 2012), due to global warming, transformation of the landscape, famine, drought, and other natural disasters affecting entire regions.

These environmental risks are the direct and indirect consequence of human behavior, and they are on the increase. Environmental risks lead to disparities and wars, and they will do so more and more as populations seek to occupy new areas. And such migration will affect us directly.

The geopolitical risk is significant in itself. After the fall of the Berlin Wall, a number of commentators claimed that liberal democracy had triumphed — that the Western world would no longer be affected by major conflict and would be sheltered from that terrible blight. There is no truth to this. Our democracies have no alternative but to live with the terrorist threat. After Al-Qaeda and Boko Haram, ISIS is a hydra that, from Iraq through Syria and now Libya, seeks to wipe us out. Even if it is now withdrawing from Syria and Iraq, and goes underground in the months to come, it is arming terrorists at the heart of our society—terrorists who kill indiscriminately in the name of a totalitarian and murderous ideology, terrorists who have made France one of their preferred targets. This threat reminds us that the world is interconnected and that we have no haven from factions that would tear it apart. We cannot remain passive, far from these theaters of operations, because they have direct consequences for our society. Nevertheless, I disagree with those who say that we should intervene everywhere and in all circumstances.

The terrorist threat that has come to strike a blow at our country profoundly affects our unity and our stability. A religious dimension has been brought into this military, political, and ideological conflict—and it is clouding the issue. Too many French citizens wrongly believe that fighting ISIS means fighting Islam.

We are confronted not only with the terrorist threat, but also with the threat of a religious war—or, at least, if we are not very careful, with the threat of conflict dictated by emotion and figments of the imagination. No task is more urgent than for us to use our powers of discernment.

Today, the state is being asked to eliminate all threats. This is a promise it cannot fulfill.

Certain politicians, both from the Left and the Right, are inclined towards saber-rattling. They propose to renounce the rule of law in order to better protect our citizens. They will not protect them any better by doing so, because they will never be able to prevent terrorist action, nor monitor every individual. However, in pursuing this path they will have given the terrorists their victory—those terrorists who want us to abandon, out of fear, what we are. Others think that by symbolically modifying the Constitution they will be able to channel the violence at work in our society. This was the subject of the unproductive and even harmful debate on the withdrawal of citizenship.

Actually, in the face of these threats, uncompromising resolve and true authority are required—at the same time accepting that these approaches cannot set everything right immediately. Building a peaceful society will take time.

The great transformation that we are currently experiencing is shaking up France's post-war landscape, and is a challenge for society.

We are experiencing a final stage in world capitalism, which, as a result of its excesses, is showing itself to be incapable of enduring. The excesses of financialization, inequalities, destruction of the environment, the inexorable increase in world population, rising geopolitical and environmental migration, the digital transformation: these are the constituent parts of a great upheaval. It requires us to act. We have probably never gone through such a time since the invention of printing and the discovery of the American continent. Such sea changes—the reinvention of social, political, and artistic boundaries, and completely new ways of thinking—were at the forefront of the Renaissance in the West. The Renaissance ushered in a rebirth at a time when Western civilization might have disappeared.

This great transformation places an obligation on us all. It is not the French way to resist global change and to content ourselves with trying to retrofit a model created for times gone by. It is not the French way to forget that which makes us what we are, to deny our principles, to flutter around like frenzied moths alarmed by the dark flame of terrorism. It is not the French way to cast doubt upon ourselves more and more each day, or to eat all our words. We French people know this well, and we are ready to reinvent our country.

CHAPTER FIVE

The France that we want

The mission to be accomplished is sizeable. We cannot embark upon it without a keen awareness of the changes taking place around us, nor without resolutely putting an end to the lethargy that has been setting in for far too long.

There are many issues to be tackled, but the most insidious of these is laxity. We are less the victims of our enemies than of our own inertia. We put up with the fact that unemployment figures have reached six million—cutting across all categories of workers, we put up with our faltering manufacturing industry, our obsolete institutional practices, our own petty divisions that solve nothing, and a thousand-and-one cases of assumed or inherited privileges that have no justification. We have become accustomed to an outmoded system of national education, to an inadequate and archaic territorial structure, and to a system of laws and regulations dating back to the nineteenth century that serves less to guarantee respect for great principles than to maintain the comfortable status quo for those who know how to skillfully exploit the system. We accept the relative inefficiency of the administration.

This situation is disheartening, not only for citizens themselves, but also for those who have a calling for public service, one of the most commendable vocations of all. They have taken this path not out of a love for the status that it bestows, but to contribute, each in their own way, to making national policies a success. In fact, their calling, their energy, and their devotion clash on a daily basis with the psychological inertia and lack of motivation that so needs to be uprooted.

We cannot give free rein to the extremists whose untenable and inconsistent promises would draw us towards an old idealistic order that never really existed. They are proposing to divert France from the direction that the world is taking, without considering what we have to lose, and above all failing to acknowledge that such a path is inconsistent with our country's mission.

We have reached a dead-end, stopped in our tracks. Strangely, we are at once stationary and frustrated by our lack of movement. Whenever we want to change anything, voices are raised against doing away with the French social model, which, despite these advocates, is a model that just doesn't work anymore. We attempt "reforms"—a word that has become such a cliché for the people of France—without daring to explain the direction or the goal. But no one is satisfied with these attempts to maintain the status quo or with gradual reforms that are not implemented. This is the paradox of France.

The system is organized to protect the existing order. There are those who content themselves with merely condemning the situation without seeking to make real changes. The existing situation—although to no one's satisfaction—is regarded, without proper analysis, as preferable to what might happen if things were changed. This France belongs to those who would maintain entrenched positions, whether relating to financial matters, to their own privileged status, or to ideologies. These same people go along with this unjust system, but at the same time complain about it and claim to find it intolerable. So, to stifle such complaints, the state, so the argument goes, just needs to spend a larger proportion of ill-conceived taxes and create further debt.

For decades, the political class has not succeeded in coming up with any solution to obstacles, inequalities, and injustice, other than a surfeit of public spending. For more than thirty years, the Right and the Left have replaced inadequate growth with public debt. They have granted relief without funding it, and have encumbered future generations with debt without resolving any of the profound imbalances. Public spending increased by 170 billion euros in five years under the previous presidency. These figures make one's head spin. By consenting to this, we have committed the gravest error: breaking with historical continuity by leaving our children an unsustainable debt burden through our lack of courage to confront reality. We are all guilty of that cowardice. A country cannot survive in the long term in a state of inertia and deception.

In this regard, history is always instructive. I often think of what the Republic of Venice must have experienced in 1453 when Constantinople fell into the hands of the Turks. After 1204, with the culmination of the Fourth Crusade, Venice consolidated its position as a maritime and trade power, as a major player on the Silk Road: a triumphant seafaring city pioneering early manufacturing methods. It had entirely neglected its hinterland, apart from some routes that enabled it to sell its merchandise at the great fairs of Champagne in France and Flanders in Belgium. The fall of Constantinople put an end to this model. The traditional silk route became less secure and more costly. At the same time, printing was invented. The ancient world seemed to be tottering.

The future of Venice was endangered, and uncertainty pervaded. It was then that Venice decided to make a clean sweep and to turn to *terra firma*, the hinterland, so neglected until then. It developed an unprecedented route with Genoa, Barcelona, and Seville. In 1492, a Genoese in the service of Spain discovered the American continent. In 1498, the Portuguese explorer Vasco de Gama arrived in Calicut, and showed that India could be reached by sea. The overland Silk Road was dead. The high seas took over, and Venice was clever enough to adapt and keen to do so. The East was replaced by the West; the sea by land; places of passage by places where roots were put down; trade moved to other routes; and farming expanded. Irrigation canals multiplied, and new talents—Palladio, Veronese,

Giorgione—reinvented the city, creating a new Venice. They were the geniuses of that new era. Venice remained powerful and did not lose its unique character.

With these changes, Venice abandoned nothing of its spirit or strength. We might even say that Venice drew the energy it needed for this transformation from its very heart. It will be the same for us.

Together we are capable of taking up the challenge offered to us by our times, by picking up the thread of a historic millennium, which saw us separate the church from the state, create the Age of Enlightenment, discover new continents, lay claim to a universal role, create a culture without precedent, and build a strong economy. Energy is needed to do that. Such energy still exists—it is deep-seated, and goes back a long way. Those in the political arena have a duty to finally release it.

Today, the victims of our failure to carefully reconsider our choices are the young; the less informed; French people of foreign origin; future generations; those at the periphery of the labor market with temporary jobs or repeated short-term contracts; those who are unable to find stable accommodation, and are waiting for public housing or are trapped in lodgings unfit for habitation or worse; single-parent and other working families who suffocate from monthly bills and can no longer carry on; those who are discriminated against; and the list goes on. Unless we overhaul our system, this multitude of victims will swell, and with it will grow the middle classes' fear that they will see their children's future downgraded.

Every day, our country is weakened by not adapting to the direction that the world is taking. It is being split apart by blatant and intolerable injustices within.

Our first duty, then, is to rebuild a just and strong France. It is our responsibility to show the French people that there is a common path forward. A way for all.

How can we do this?

Like France in 1945 at the time of the National Council of Resistance, we must fundamentally realign our ways of thinking, acting, and evolving.

We have to move from a passive France, where choices are made by others, to a France that makes its own choices. What we want is to control our own destiny, both individually and collectively. The striking injustice that we decry stems from the fact that some have choices and others do not—that some French people are able to choose their children's schools, their place of residence, their jobs, and their vacation destinations, whereas for others those choices are made for them by their circumstances.

What unites the French people is their true and sincere passion for equality. In my view, they are justifiably indignant about the continuing disgrace of inequality, cynicism, and social iniquities. We dream of being a nation of people who are not carbon copies of each other, but who have equal access to rights and, more fundamentally, opportunities. Our current system no longer allows us to seek equality. As a result of higher expenditure and more regulation, we have paralyzed and then dragged down our entire society to the lowest common denominator, and have brought it to a standstill.

For thirty years, both the Left and the Right have continuously defended a system that has promoted uniformity, prevented differentiation, and led to commodification. I do not believe in an "egalitarianism" that does not tolerate the success of others. At the same time, the Left and the Right have created entitlements without a thought for how to fund them, devoid of substance, while making out that this is what progress means now. But what should we make of a fundamental right to housing in a country in which millions of people are inadequately housed? True equality is not written in laws. Instead, it places every person at the same point of departure—in practice. It gives every individual the tools to succeed at school and at work, and provides health services, and opportunities for mobility and security. That is what politics owes the French people. Not promises of a single model that operates across the board, but the same opportunities for all, at every stage of their lives.

We should also move from an economy of "playing catch-up" to one of innovation. Today, we no longer have the "great projects" economy of the "Thirty Glorious Years".

Our goal should not be to imitate products conceived abroad, but to innovate in our own country. The strength and power of the emerging model lie in an alliance that business is in a position to forge with millions of consumers.

It would bring about a strongly decentralized and more horizontal economy, in which the consumer is first and foremost a creator of value. Nevertheless, innovation is not progress in itself. To innovate just for the sake of innovation is like wandering aimlessly in the dark. What counts is the use to which we put innovation. It is the direction we give it. It should not leave us in open-eyed wonder. It should be tackled lucidly, in a clear-headed manner, to ensure that technology serves economic, social, and ecological progress, and allows all of us greater freedom of action.

Corporate protectionism should give way to safeguards for individuals. The members of the National Council of Resistance who forged the 1945 consensus took into account sickness, accidents in the workplace, and pensions. To tackle these issues, they created social protection based on a single principle: society would protect from sickness, old age, and work-related accidents only those holding jobs. That protection would vary according to the worker category and the business sector, and sometimes according to the occupation. Nevertheless, they did not anticipate the emergence of a society of rapid and ruthless change, of deindustrialization, and the resulting instability. They did not imagine that unemployment would one day be the lot of 10 per cent of the labor force. They were unable to conceive of the fragmentation of the world of work, the growing place of temporary employment, and of, in short, a post-employee economy. The reality is that social-protection measures no longer cover an ever-growing number of our compatriots.

So as to address this de facto injustice, and to support each and every person in a more insecure world, new social protections must no longer be granted according to the status of individual French citizens. They must be organized in a more transparent and universal manner, with rights, but also obligations, for all.

We must move from a centralized model to one that enables each person to be engaged. Who can seriously believe that the best way is to control everything from Paris? To solve different problems with the same solution? To treat citizens as subjects, rather than to consider them as actors in their own right? French society abounds in vitality, but that vitality is taken not only from traditional channels—Paris, the major government departments, the elite universities, and large corporations. It also stems, and probably even more vigorously so, from deprived neighborhoods, from rural France, from the young, from local authorities, and from small businesses. Our country's energy is our good fortune.

The state can no longer, as it once did, meet this century's challenges by issuing unilateral fiats. Hence, on subjects as crucial as environmental change, everyone needs to be on board. It will be the businesses, the employees, the consumers, and the civil servants who will bring about the transformation of our manufacturing model. We must therefore, without delay, afford everyone the power to act and succeed. To be responsible. To be engaged in their future.

We have a choice of two approaches. Either an approach

that offers a few remedies purporting to be radical that will do no more than postpone clinical death if they don't exacerbate the illness. Or one that consists of organizing an in-depth restructuring of our model on the basis of some carefully selected priorities—to rebuild an overarching social and economic equilibrium.

The time for small and expedient accommodations on these matters that impact the lives of our compatriots is long past. We simply have to change our way of thinking.

To reconcile France's polarities means responding to the French people's desire for equitable prosperity: liberty for each person to be creative, to be mobile, and to be enterprising; equality of opportunity to achieve those aims; and social fraternity, especially for the weakest.

What keeps France united stems from both acceptance and rejection: acceptance of diverse origins and destinies; and rejection of fatalism. From this standpoint emanates our determination to provide independence for all and to offer a place in our society for every woman and man. A dream of creating a nation made up not of people that are all the same, but of people with equal rights.

This mission will take ten years. It has to begin right now.

CHAPTER SIX

Investing in our future

In order to thrive, to act fairly towards the vulnerable in our society, and to retain our ranking in the family of nations, there is only one path for us to take: to re-establish manufacturing, and by so doing to create the conditions for a new prosperity in our country. Deindustrialization in France is one of the causes of our adversity. The challenge is not to recreate post-war industrial France. That would make no sense. We must be fired with enthusiasm to reinvigorate the industrial dream that is at the heart of our history and our identity.

That dream was the realm of the state in the days of Colbert, it was in the forefront of the industrial revolution under Napoleon III, and it was further developed under the fourth Republic and in the first years of the fifth Republic. It has never ceased to inspire our country's entrepreneurs and workers. It is at the very heart of our identity, because France has never regarded itself as anything other than a creative, inventive, innovative country playing a significant role in the advancement of humankind.

In the light of that aspiration, which goes back more than two hundred years, today's realities are particularly harsh. Since 2000, we have eliminated almost 900,000 manufacturing jobs, and industry's share of our Gross Domestic Product has fallen from 17 per cent to 12 per cent. There is therefore no more urgent task than reforging our industrial potential, which is currently jeopardized and may remain so for some time to come.

Rekindling our manufacturing dream is also a social imperative. There is no point in simply asserting that in France we are concerned with not abandoning the most vulnerable if, at the same time, we let French industry drift and go downhill without lifting a finger. Real prosperity is created first and foremost through the production of goods and services. The wealth generated can then be shared. Without production there can be no "social model".

A precondition for attaining that goal is choosing the right economic policy. Instead, for thirty years and until recently, we have chosen to substitute public spending for economic growth. We have been very generous with social benefits, but we have never tackled the roots of mass unemployment. We have supported housing benefits, but have not sufficiently kept abreast of construction needs. In short, we have built a palliative rather than a productive model for expenditure. Today, that model has run out of steam. Our levels of debt bar us from accumulating an even-greater deficit to finance our current expenditure.

Our rate of compulsory levies prohibits us from raising taxes any further. Having said that, does this mean that the state must make indiscriminate cuts in spending and withdraw from public involvement in the economy? That would be just as absurd. More than ever, we need to invest in schools, healthcare, and energy transition, to name but a few. These are domains in which the state could do better, but where nothing can be achieved without the state's involvement.

I have therefore always been uncomfortable with the debate that pits the partisans of "revitalizing" the economy against those advocating "austerity". I believe that this dichotomy is misguided. The first group believe that it is sufficient to increase deficits as a way of supporting our economy without taking into account public finances. The other group holds that it is sufficient to make spending cuts and reduce deficits at any price, in order to boost growth. Both are wrong. Just as it would not be appropriate to aim to balance our public accounts in the current context of transition, so it would not be healthy to remain unconcerned about levels of public expenditure and their effectiveness, as well as levels of taxes and other statutory contributions.

I favor pursuing a policy of reducing our public expenditure. Rather than focusing on the deficit, our public accounts should be steered according to public-expenditure targets. We can do this without weakening growth or calling into question necessary social protection. We spend the equivalent of 56 per cent of our national wealth on this area, whereas the average expenditure for the Eurozone, with largely similar levels of protection, stands at 49 per cent. We can resolve to achieve this at a steady but sensible pace by aiming for more efficient public spending.

We must do this at the same time as prioritizing real savings and ensuring that all stakeholders have a sense of responsibility, rather than the government merely shaving budgets over and over again.

Keeping in mind our priorities and the need to be fair, all sectors—the state and its agencies, local authorities, and the social welfare agencies—must play their part. Is it logical to refrain from reforming the allocation of 18 billion euros of personalized housing benefits, when they benefit recipients less than they do property owners, and feed into hikes in real-estate prices? Is it appropriate to let operating costs continue to rise (despite decentralization initiatives), while investments shrink? Is it relevant to maintain an unemployment benefit cap in excess of 6,000 euros per month, when our system has recorded a deficit in the order of 4 billion euros? Alternative ways of addressing these questions will allow us to reduce compulsory levies.

What matters in the short term is to take strategic decisions that will put us on the right path. Unlike the dogmatic partisans of economic "recovery", we need to undertake major structural reforms, systematically review public policies, and resolutely pursue the goal of reducing futile spending. And, unlike the dogmatic partisans of "austerity", we have to accept that our economy has vital needs in a number of domains, and is still struggling to recover from the economic and financial crisis. It would be absurd to endanger our future growth just to reduce the budget deficit by 0.1 per cent of GDP, and not to take advantage of historically low interest rates—thereby failing to finance investments that would be profitable for our country. I therefore believe that we must in the very near future conduct a policy that promotes our economic growth, comprising two pillars of equal importance: public investment in key domains, and a sustainable reduction in running costs.

I consider three domains to be priorities for public investment.

The first is "human capital", as the economists call it—that is, education and training. Once more, investment in schools, in higher education and research, but also in continuing education, is absolutely critical. It is the only way to give France the means to achieve its ambitions in the coming decades. In this domain, we are experiencing the effects of a delay that is costing us dearly. It is making us less productive, less innovative, and less competitive. It exacerbates mass unemployment and inequalities. Even from a strictly financial point of view, it is harmful, because insufficient investment in schools or in training compels us to spend even more to repair the damage done. To invest in human capital is also to finance French innovation. In the field of healthcare, for example, we have formidable innovative capacity, particularly in our public hospitals and laboratories, and in our companies.

Currently, we support these institutions with a tax credit envied all over the world because it enables companies to offset a portion of their investments in R&D against their taxes. Nevertheless, our system is still recalcitrant about allowing innovation to flourish. The procedures take too long, and the rules are too complicated. It was for this reason that the researchers who conceptualized the artificial heart—a world first for France—almost took their project abroad in the face of our complex system. Once more, we must not only invest, but also drastically simplify practices in order to support and encourage, rather than to restrict and hinder.

The second domain that needs to be a priority for state investment is environmental transition. If certain people are allowed to continue to promote their own short-term interests at any cost, we are headed for failure. This is clear in the domain of energy—where responsible citizens and businesses are not automatically compensated by free-market forces. The improved insulation and heating of existing homes, and the wider use of electricity requires public investment. But this is also true in the domain of agro-ecology, where an individual farmer does not necessarily have the means to undertake on his own a transition to a new model that might require calling upon stakeholders across the whole energy sector. It applies also to infrastructure and transportation, to enable the whole country to be better served. There, too, we will need the government to initiate, coordinate, and mobilize all our resources, while sharing long-term plans with private stakeholders. In these fields, the state must get involved and send the right messages to the right stakeholders. It must also invest in and foster innovation, step up environmental taxes, reliefs, and schemes, and support all those businesses, large and small, that will lead us towards a low-carbon, environmentally friendly economy.

The third domain is the deployment of fiber optics throughout France. After the railways, electricity, television, and the telephone, this is a national project like almost none other in our history. It is particularly vital for the most isolated areas. Today, fiber optics are indispensable for rapid modernization across our entire economy and to enable it to turn a crucial technological corner within just a few years. In my capacity as minister, I actively guided the current policy for fiber optics deployment by telecommunications operators. I am now aware that for the most far-flung rural areas, the state itself, in addition to co-financing, must also be uncompromisingly committed, particularly where the operators fail to step up, and it must promote innovative solutions, including by way of satellite.

What I want to institute is a five-year public-investment plan. This is the only way to meet the longstanding needs of the whole country and all of our economic actors, and give them the necessary long-term view. I am hoping for swift European initiatives in this area, but I have no wish to wait for unforeseeable and potentially slow decisions.

Of course, budgetary regulation and a reduction of public expenditure must be encouraged in order to reduce our permanent deficits, which are an indicator of the dysfunctions in our administrative bureaucracy. However, regulation must not prevent us from seizing opportunities. This is why I stress in national and European debates that we need to separate the undeniable need for savings and efficiency in our operating costs, on the one hand, from the need to invest in and modernize our economy, on the other.

Europe clearly has a decisive role in this regard. If we want to build our country's future, we must carry out radical reforms at home, while investing both in France and in Europe.

In parallel, investment initiated by companies themselves is paramount. It is in this way that innovation and the development of new activities will enable us to move towards a robust growth model. Twenty years ago, France lost the battle for robotics by halting investments in that field, believing that this would protect jobs. It was not the case. On the contrary. Germany, for its part, has five times as many robots in its factories, and has been able to keep many more jobs in industry. They now have an unemployment rate that is almost half ours. Today, France must ensure that its economy fully embraces the opportunities presented by innovation and the digital age.

Businesses, large and small, artisanal or industrial, should build up their profit margins to facilitate greater investment. For that purpose, they need a long-term view and stability. They have to be able to make future plans and investment forecasts, devise their company policy, and set out to conquer new markets. In France today, companies spend too much time trying to understand continual changes in the laws. While our economy is being transformed at great speed, and while the economic climate is increasingly uncertain, public authorities have a responsibility not to be a source of concern and paralysis.

Sometimes even positive measures are ineffective because instability makes firms hesitant. How can one explain the fifty amendments enacted in the Labor Code since 2000? How can one justify the fact that even in the course of a five-year presidential term the regulations in a given sector or tax obligations can be changed over and over again?

So let us establish some basic principles: once a reform has been initiated, we should not modify the measures taken, but should allow them to be applied before we assess them; let us make a commitment not to modify a particular tax several times in the course of a five-year presidential term. Whole sections of our economy have been disrupted by changes in regulations that have weighed down business activity, despite good reasons for the changes. In several sectors of our economy—such as housing, agriculture, and the hotel and restaurant sectors—we have changed the regulations far too often. I do not want us to add new rules before reviewing those that are already in place and are not proving useful. Let us invite stakeholders and all French citizens to identify regulations that have become outdated. We also require sound judgment and consistency from public officials in the field.

In a dairy that I visited a few kilometers from Aurillac, the young farmer managing it told me that two years earlier he had been required to invest in a footbath at the entrance to the cowshed. The same state department then reversed their instruction a few months later, and informed him that the footbath should be dismantled because it had created problems to do with hygiene. The regulation had been promulgated without explanation, and then amended, again without explanation. That little joke cost him three months' income. How can the state retain its credibility in such circumstances? How likely are businesses to invest in the appropriate improvements when they are undermined in a manner that is both inexplicable and authoritarian?

To invest in innovation, companies need to reconstitute their profit margins and thus reduce costs of labor, energy, and capital. In that respect, the current five-year presidential term will have marked a turning point, particularly with regard to labor costs. The CICE (Tax Credit for Competitiveness and Employment) and the Responsibility and Solidarity Pact will have returned to companies some room for maneuver, and will have stopped the hemorrhaging of jobs.

In this domain, I want matters to be clear. I wish to reduce those business levies that are detrimental to competitiveness, and to support investment in manufacturing. To achieve this, amongst other things, I will transform the CICE into a scheme for the reduction of contributions, and I will decide other ways to reduce or eliminate the amount of employer payments. Savings on public expenditure, and tax incentives—on pollution and consumption, in particular—will be established to finance this strategy.

Under those conditions, businesses will be able both to hire staff and invest, which are the two priorities for our economy.

As regards innovation, stable regulations and reductions in contributions are admittedly not the be-all and end-all. We have to encourage and develop our entrepreneurial forces. We often talk about start-ups, and implicit in this term is a lot more than a passing fad. A new model is emerging for business and entrepreneurs—the catalyst of economic transformation and cultural change.

Up to now, France has harbored a paradox that could be fatal for our future. On the one hand, we stigmatize failure; on the other hand, we marginalize success. The fear of failure is etched into the minds of our children. At school, we compel children to conform to a single model of excellence, and some fail. The result is that our young people lose self-confidence, and they become scared to take risks. This is why I believe that it is incumbent upon us to impress on people's minds that if a person fails it is first and foremost because they have tried. And that if a person has failed they have a considerable advantage over someone who has never tried: they have acquired experience. At the same time, we have to place a value on success—it is the other side of the same coin. We have to learn to salute and celebrate people who succeed in all walks of life. So let us shine a light on all French successes, whether entrepreneurial, social, intellectual, sporting, or cultural.

In my opinion, there are two simple prerequisites for entrepreneurship to succeed and develop in France. First, a tax system that rewards risk-taking and wealth acquired through talent, work, and innovation, rather than through dividends and property investment. Our tax system—and I include here the current wealth tax—should no longer penalize those who achieve success in their own lifetimes and invest in businesses and innovation.

Then we need a system of financing that enables our businesses to raise large amounts of capital rapidly. That is indispensable in a knowledge economy.

Why is it that a firm such as Uber is now the leading taxi company in France, when we have French competitors offering more or less the same service? It is because Uber has already managed to raise tens of billions of dollars, whereas the French firms have only raised tens of millions. Clearly, the problem in France is a lack of fast access to major capital funding.

To conclude, there will be no investment in the future of our country if the state does not guarantee equitable protection and require the same compliance with regulations by all. For this, we need a competition policy—a crucial instrument that, in my view, we have wrongly, too often, and artificially set against manufacturing policy. The rules of competition enable the smallest and newest businesses to enter a market if they fight for a place, work hard, and innovate. Without competition, room is reserved exclusively for those who have been around for a long time and who come to understandings and accommodations with one another. Competition protects against collusion, and fosters freedom — it is essential.

How can farmers innovate or invest in transforming their methods and equipment if we do not protect them from the supermarkets and if we do not make sure there is fair competition to ensure that certain major retail chains do not collude to reduce the producer's profit margin? Competition is indispensable for innovation.

The state also has a responsibility to provide a long-term vision.

To elaborate by using the same example: in order to survive, farmers often need to modernize and to purchase equipment in order to produce at lower cost and to increase the value of what they produce. As in every economic sector, farmers need stability to stay committed over a period of years. For them, particularly, if the market is not regulated to assist them to overcome price fluctuations, it becomes problematic to invest. The state must guarantee stability in the long-term, through sectoral agreements to protect crucial innovation.

Unfair competition from foreign countries obviously hampers innovation and the hiring of staff. It is also vital to ensure compliance with the rules of the game and, along with the European Union, to vigorously combat any unfair competition. This is where European economic sovereignty is critical. When giant corporations from Asia and America do not play by the rules of the game, and when a strategic sector needs to be protected, public authorities must have their say and must assume their responsibilities. In my capacity as minister, I made every effort to ensure that the European Union would get its voice heard by the Chinese players in the steel industry and would better protect the iron and steel businesses in our country. I defended artisan workers and small-business owners in the face of competition from the Internet giants, and even more importantly pleaded the case for the new economy to be conceived of as a growth opportunity for them.

This means lifting the obstacles that hinder the development of these businesses, beginning with the multiplicity of rules and levies that are not imposed on powerful corporations such as Google, Apple, Facebook, and Amazon.

Certain sectors cannot be left to the whims of the market. The protection of our national sovereignty must be tackled with our eyes open, and the full range of instruments available for government intervention must be mobilized: direct support, government shareholdings, authorizing inward investment ... As regards defense-related sectors, there are obvious strategic challenges for our military sovereignty. The state directly supports the development of military programs, in particular in its role as customer. In this sector, it must retain its equity in several key enterprises, and closely monitor changes in the shareholders of private companies. When raw materials or energy are the issue, the state must also be on the front line, because the stakes are at once our country's energy independence, robust environmental choices, operating costs for all our businesses, and purchasing power for our citizens. This is why more recently the state has been deemed to have a legitimate role in restructuring the nuclear sector, which alone enables the production of decarbonized electricity at particularly competitive prices. And it is also why it will be legitimate in the future to support the diversification of our energy mix, so as not to be dependent on a single technology.

It is for these reasons that I could never accept the ready-made solutions of adherents either to the doctrine of Colbert's mercantilism, on the one hand, or to that of the liberals, on the other. For the former, the state gives direction, decides on everything, leads, and implements: these people wish for the return of the *Plan Calcul*. For the latter, the market cannot be wrong, and the best industrial policy would be to have no industrial policy at all. For my part, I subscribe to neither of these solutions: not the arguable efficiency of the former, nor the dangerous over-simplified approach of the latter.

Fair protection and ensuring compliance with rules is thus the role of the state if we want our businesses to invest in our future. The challenge is immense. For ten years now, France has been contending with the aftermath of the global economic crisis that began in

2008. We have been obsessed, sometimes justifiably, by short-term considerations, trade or budgetary deficits, margins or interest rates. In many respects, these indicators have improved: we have reduced our budget deficit and considerably improved our competitiveness. However, in reality we have been improvising with globalization for thirty years, without finding our rightful place — that of an economy of excellence, entrepreneurship, and innovation, at the forefront of great digital, cultural, and environmental transformations.

CHAPTER SEVEN

Producing in France and saving the planet

In order to achieve economic success in the twenty-first century, we have to offer a response to the many environmental challenges we are facing. For example, how we might enable ten billion human beings to inhabit our planet without degrading it and without sacrificing our standard of living. The environment is not simply one issue amongst many, nor an item to be ticked off on a political agenda. It has become front and center. It is at the heart of our daily lives because it affects our food, our health, our housing, and our means of transport. It impacts our model for development and, more fundamentally, the longevity of our civilization.

The fight for the environment is above all a political one. Just as in the previous century there were those who chose to ignore the growing gulf between social classes, so too we still have climate-change skeptics who, whether by conviction or by design, deny the very existence of global warming. In the United States and in Europe, certain heads of state or candidates for that position openly defend such a thesis. To hear them tell it, we can continue to live, to consume, and to produce as we do now. The most accomplished experts, however, such as Jean Jouzel, have made the matter very plain, and have never been contradicted.

It is essential to continue to raise awareness, to make matters clear, and to demonstrate that we no longer have a choice and that we urgently need to speed up the changes that we have begun.

At the international level, we need to begin by defining our goals in order to reverse the continuous rise in greenhouse-gas emissions. A first step was taken at the COP21 United Nations Climate Change Conference held in Paris in 2015, which enabled an agreement to be reached on limiting global warming to two degrees Celsius by the year 2100.

The ability to reach that consensus is testimony to the ever-growing numbers who believe that our planet is truly in danger and that action must be taken. Since the beginning of the industrial age, the earth's average temperature has, in fact, risen by one degree Celsius, with consequences that are already noticeable: every year is hotter than the last. We are spending more and more money to extract the last drops of energy from almost defunct sources than we are to advance the sources of the future. A seventh continent, made of plastic, has begun to emerge from the oceans. On the one hand, we are wasting a third of the food that we produce, and, on the other hand, obesity is rampant. Devices that we use for a year or two will take centuries to decompose naturally.

These trends are only accelerating. If nothing is done to reduce greenhouse-gas emissions, the average temperature of the planet could increase by more than four degrees between now and 2100. That translates into a considerable rise in sea level, the disappearance of a number of islands and even whole areas of countries such as Bangladesh, as well as the proliferation of extreme weather events.

The environmental consequences would be disastrous. The social consequences would be no less so, because the number of climate refugees could reach several hundred million, with implications for the movement of populations and for the peace of the earth. By way of example, Syria recorded the worst drought in its history between 2006 and 2011. Attributed to climate change, it is considered one of the contributing factors to the war. We should never forget that the challenge of climate change first threatens the most vulnerable, the poorest, the youngest, and future generations.

Record temperatures reached in 2016, probably the hottest year in recorded history until then, remind us of the urgent need to act. That is why I am amongst those who salute the work done by France to reach the Paris Agreement, which enabled an extraordinary mobilization of all strata of civil society throughout the world: states, businesses, trade unions, associations, local and public authorities, and religious movements.

Nevertheless, a great deal remains to be done. This is even truer since Donald Trump was elected. Europe must make its voice heard on the world stage to ensure that the commitments already pledged at COP21, including by the United States, are fulfilled. It is all the more important because these undertakings are insufficient to put us on a trajectory to reach the goal of a limit of two degrees Celsius, and will need to be revised upwards. A comparable international mobilization is needed to protect biodiversity and the oceans, in keeping with the adoption of a new Agenda for Sustainable Development. And there, too, our country has a key role to play. We have the second-largest maritime space in the world. We are the only European country classified amongst the eighteen richest countries in the world in terms of biodiversity, and one of the ten countries in the world that host the greatest number of endangered species. Finally, we are a member of all the major global governance authorities, including the G7, the G20, and the United Nations Security Council.

We have a duty to spearhead and defend this action. We need to bring together our state agencies with responsibility for these issues and to locate them in our overseas territories, which are the best place to showcase these challenges. For it is in these territories that we see the full range of France's biodiversity and its climate — a global France.

It is there that we encounter the reality of the challenges that France faces. It is from there that we must establish our base and spread our message. Not from Paris.

However, we also need to act in an exemplary manner ourselves. That is why I want to place the new initiatives to protect the environment at the heart of policy to be implemented by France over the coming years, and at the heart of the policies to be developed by the European Union.

In doing so, we will have the legitimacy to be heard in the councils of the world. I am optimistic. The new environmental protection that we have to put in place in no way runs counter to the new economy that we wish to promote. It is actually one of its essential components. It offers an economic opportunity for those businesses that prove capable of providing new responses, including building houses that consume less energy than they produce, developing organic farming methods, and so on. Public investment and support are essential to achieve this. At the same time, it is also an opportunity for our society, because these solutions will enable us to eat better, to be healthier, to breathe less-polluted air—in short, to have a better life.

Far from being contradictory, economic imperatives and environmental imperatives will, in the future, be increasingly complementary.

Everyone knows of the exploits of an airplane called Solar Impulse, which circled the globe using only solar energy. Less well known is the fact that scientific advances in new fields of chemistry made it possible. France holds all the cards to be a world leader in environmental innovation.

Tomorrow, "clean-tech" companies will be one of the central pillars of the global economy.

The operating costs of solar technologies have dropped by more than 80 per cent since 2009 and should plummet by around 60 per cent between now and 2025, which will make this the cheapest method of generating electricity. With renewable sources, such as wind and solar energy, we know that one of the fundamental problems is transporting energy over long distances and storing it. These are precisely the issues at the core of continuing work at a number of large groups and start-ups all over the world. And French companies rank among the very best.

Moreover, the oceans are and will remain one of the hubs of our energy transformation. Renewable marine energies will be further developed and will facilitate the diversification of our manufacturing.

As regards energy efficiency, we know that the main focus is to reduce energy consumption by insulating buildings and equipping them with efficient heating systems. Progress is underway: condensing boilers have become the norm, heat pumps and wood heating have a considerably higher output, while construction companies are working to make roof and wall insulation less onerous.

We are leaving behind us the oil-and-gas age, and moving into an era that increasingly relies on electrical power, such as for public or individual transportation. We are seeing extraordinary developments in electric vehicles, with a diversification of models, a growing increase in battery life, and the halving of their cost in less than ten years. Innovation is also on the march in terms of our practices—the use of digital tools that enable cars and bicycles to be shared, and transport to be better planned.

The new ecological economy will have a conservation impact, too—on our land, our rivers, and even our oceans, which are currently blighted by veritable islands of plastic. The same goes for the quality of the air that we breathe in our homes and in our offices.

Due to atmospheric pollution, the life expectancy of a thirty-year-old is reduced on average by fifteen months in urban areas and by nine months in rural areas, and the cost of air pollution in France has been assessed by some studies at more than one hundred billion euros a year.

The transformation of our factories is already well under way, at their own initiative. Over the past twenty years, in countries such as France, it is the factories that have reduced their greenhouse-gas emissions the most. And their emissions of toxic particles such as sulfur or dioxin have been almost entirely eradicated. The factory of the future will enable us to take further steps by transforming heat into a source of energy for our cities, by repurposing obsolete consumer products and giving them a new life—in short, by designing a circular economy that throws away nothing and recycles everything.

Because France has in its ranks highly qualified researchers in chemistry, physics, and the biological sciences, and a broad and diverse range of businesses—large groups, small and medium-sized enterprises that are experiencing strong growth, and a network of high-performing start-ups—it has all the advantages to position itself strongly in the field of clean technologies.

Now is the time to give a strong political boost to all economic partners to signal a great national mobilization in the service of green technologies.

And we must be careful not to miss opportunities at this crucial time. At the outset of the twenty-first century, we failed to embrace the shift to the new information and communication technologies. That digital revolution is now dominated by giant U.S. corporations. In the five coming years, we must position ourselves amongst the world champions of clean technologies. These are the issues at stake for the planet and for our industrial sovereignty. We cannot now manufacture in France in the same way as we once did. Millions of jobs and billions in savings are at stake.

In parallel, the financial center in Paris is putting in place a strategy and the appropriate regulatory environment conducive to it becoming the global leader in green finance. With this perspective, I believe that Europe would have everything to gain by adopting an environmental tax policy that prioritizes responsible conduct by our citizens and our businesses, and that allows the tax burden on labor to be reduced.

The new environmental approach will characterize our world all the more because the twenty-first century will increasingly become the age of cities. Obviously, cities have a major role to play in taking up the various environmental challenges. And, in that regard, we are well positioned to assert our strengths—first and foremost because we created a historical model of a sustainable city, even before that term was invented, which we can now draw upon.

In comparison with most cities in America or Asia, European cities are compact. They were not built around the use of automobiles, and rarely suffer from urban sprawl. It is within the compact city that decarbonized public transport can be developed and smart-energy networks established. Currently, the countries of Europe are often at the forefront—putting in place smart networks, building entire neighborhoods that produce more energy than they use, developing car- and bicycle-sharing schemes, or simply by organizing new systems that prioritize on-foot mobility for pedestrians and hikers.

Such cities are more ordered, but at the same time have a more human dimension. They encourage people to get together and create new connections between residents. Far from being an environment of constraint, the new environment that we want to develop is one of contentment, the rediscovered pleasure of living in a calmer city where residents play an increasingly active role over time. We see this through the communities being formed to regulate energy consumption or to build shared city gardens.

France has the advantage of having world experts with know-how in the field of sustainable cities. It is not by chance that Paris is known for the density of its subway network, and that Paris and Lyon were among the first cities to open the way for bicycle sharing.

This urban transformation should benefit everyone, and, in particular, those most in need. Under no circumstances should the new smart city become a paradise reserved for those who can afford to live in it. This requires investment in public transport, the opening up of less affluent neighborhoods, and public and private investment in urban planning. The new smart city must enable those of modest means to live in pleasant surroundings and to move around at the lowest possible cost.

The new environmental approach will also enable us to transform our countryside. It has the potential to be a factor in the robust development of our agriculture if, once again, we are able to seize the opportunity. First, because diversification, particularly when directed towards energy production and recovery, is a source of income growth for farmers; second, because the many short-term crises—in supplies of products (such as milk, meat, and cereals); in sanitation (mad-cow disease, avian flu); and related to the environment (pesticides, nitrates)—bear witness to a highly compromised agricultural model.

On the one hand, farmers, like all French people, simply wish to make a living from their work. They do not make excessive requests for more state aid, and they just want their work to be compensated at a fair price. On the other hand, consumers expect food that is healthier and more balanced. They rely on French farmers to provide them with that. In the future, we must create a new social pact with the world of agriculture to enable the greatest number of people to have access to quality food, at affordable prices, while guaranteeing farmers a decent income. This social pact will be predicated on farming that is both more competitive and more sustainable. My belief is that these requirements are not contradictory. However, our farming sector and the food-processing industry must be able to grasp this opportunity. We must see to it that the large-scale retail sector also participates.

To this end, we have to better regulate the various sectors, by way of contracts that allow a fair price to be determined: a price that enables the producer, the manufacturer, and the retailer to generate income and to grow their businesses; this presupposes transparency in all their profit margins, as well as multi-year agreements that enable everyone to plan for the future and not be subject to price volatility. We must all understand that our food sovereignty and thus our future depend on our farmers.

In this context, the new Common Agricultural Policy (CAP) 2020 will constitute an important platform by which to implement more effective regulation that will foster progress in safeguarding against excessive price fluctuations.

Practices must also change. Farmers must be more committed to adding value to and raising the profile of their products in subsequent stages of the supply chain. They should be assisted and encouraged in that. A few kilometers from the commune of Château-Thierry in the *département* of Aisne, I met the man in charge of a family pig-

and-poultry farm that might have closed down a long time ago. With fifty sows and the intensity of the crisis of recent years, he didn't stand a chance. However, he invested in quality stock, and decided to process the products himself and sell them directly, cutting out intermediaries. Not only is he making a living today, but his three children will be able to take over the farm and continue to diversify.

Some winegrowers have already made this change, by moving away from mass production—in southern France, for example—and instituting Controlled Designation of Origin. Winegrowers who were about to lose everything discovered a new economic dynamic, which also brought in its wake a boost for tourism. What has been done for winegrowing should be implemented for all sectors, so that we see producers gaining market share both in France and abroad.

UNESCO recently classified "The Gastronomic Meal of the French" on the List of the Intangible Cultural Heritage of Humanity. By making use of that brand image, openings are possible for all our agricultural products if we prove ourselves capable of moving upmarket. Here, too, as in all domains, French production does not succeed by decree, but must be earned day by day.

The French are amongst the citizens most concerned about the future of our planet, but when it comes to changing habits, they hardly reach the European average in terms of recycling or renovation work on buildings to improve energy efficiency.

Concern for the environment cannot be reduced to

debates between experts or discussions at large international conferences. It emerges firstly in the decisions and initiatives taken on a daily basis by households, companies, local authorities, and NGOs: recycling, selecting consumer products with certificates of sustainability, the supply of sustainable raw materials, the manufacture of repairable rather than disposable eco-designed products, mobility choices, and insulation improvements. The public authorities are responsible for creating means and incentives, but they cannot make decisions in place of actors on the ground.

Everyone must be allowed to find their own way of engaging with this issue, while being fully invested in decisions made at state level.

CHAPTER EIGHT

Educating all our children

At the heart of the regeneration of our production system are investments in our future and the use of twenty-first century methods. The school is the first battleground in transforming the country and enabling everyone to find their place in the great changes taking shape.

We must reject everything that leads to categorizing French people according to their different origins. Such a rejection is the French way, and it has made us a great nation. But we must not content ourselves with that—we must fight to ensure that access to knowledge and to culture is shared more effectively.

Over the last century, our school system—from pre-school through middle to high school—and on to our universities, including the *grandes écoles*, has not let us down. It is not by chance that France became a great scientific, technological, commercial, military, cultural, and political power. It is thanks to excellent French tuition that we enjoyed outstanding success over such a long period. We provided access to education for all, welcomed new communities, and considerably increased the numbers of Baccalaureate and higher-education graduates in our country.

Now, however, the performance of our schools has become mediocre. Our educational system maintains inequalities, and even accentuates them, instead of alleviating them. French school students lack confidence in themselves and in their educational institutions. Their parents are worried. Worse still, teachers are fighting the indifference of a bureaucratic system that does not recognize either their efforts or their merits.

One-fifth of students leave primary school without being able to read, write, or count. The first victims of this catastrophe are the poorest, who are often children of immigrants. They fare no better at middle school or high school, despite the development of technological and vocational tracks at those institutions. Furthermore, those track programs have not achieved the success of the apprenticeship system of our German neighbors.

There is almost no chance for students who still cannot read or write by fifth grade to subsequently gain access to training for a profession, and to later find their place in society.

As for our system of higher education, it selects students with strong potential, and separates them from the others. The first group have the opportunity to be admitted to the *grandes écoles* and to obtain the best university education.

The others, who have the greatest need for support, are very often left to enroll blindly in university programs developed without the necessary thought or effort.

Many misguided educational reforms have been set in motion, the latest of which reshuffled school timetables—without regard for the fact that they are an important part of children's daily lives and make a significant contribution to the proper functioning of our schools. We have improvised—first withdrawing basic training for teachers and then restoring it, without setting any goals. We increased and then reduced resources, without generating any results or assessing the consequences. The Left and the Right were, in turn, agents of that failure, which has now turned France, the fifth-richest country in the world, into a mediocre nation in the acquisition of basic competencies. This is true for the acquisition of fundamental knowledge in mathematics, as well as a command of written and spoken English, and many other disciplines.

For too many years, the state has shied away from radical transformation. It has not even been possible to raise new questions, and this has deprived us of original ideas and impeded our effectiveness. The future of our country's children, in particular the disadvantaged—given that three million French people live below the poverty line—calls for much more than minimal reforms, minor adjustments in resources, or discussions about this or that program ...

One revolution that we truly need is the transformation of our schools. There are three lines of action.

———

First, in the primary school. Because that is where inequalities take root, and where we can have the greatest impact. In France, public investment in primary schools is noticeably lower than the average for developed countries. For as long as we do not attain better results in our primary schools, the situation in middle schools, where we seek to integrate a population in great need, will not improve. Let us therefore establish a better performing and more equitable kindergarten and elementary-school system as our principal goal.

This will be attained through an ambitious plan of reinvestment in our primary schools, chiefly intended for kindergartens situated in the priority educational zones, where we will cut class sizes in half. Investment in the training and support of teachers is also essential, particularly in certain specific urban and rural regions.

This also requires an investment in non-teaching personnel, and the improvement of healthcare at school. Many children who complete elementary school cannot read and write because they have problems of vision, hearing, or other health problems that are diagnosed too late. If identified at the outset, such problems could be addressed, and the necessary care provided. This will be my priority, and I will finance it mainly by reassessing a number of the recent futile and costly reforms.

Early schooling, especially for children from disadvantaged backgrounds, has a widely recognized positive effect on language acquisition and a more extensive vocabulary, a prerequisite for learning to read and write. This early-schooling strand will be developed.

I am also keen to revise school catchment areas, so as to open up deprived neighborhoods and to fight the social and scholastic inevitability that permeates from the earliest age. This will involve redefining and clarifying rules for the allocation of students, placing greater value on schools in difficult neighborhoods by implementing innovative and special pedagogical practices, and providing the relevant transportation.

As for middle schools, we will re-establish the classes that were taught in different European languages to open the minds of our young people to participatory citizenship. We will re-establish bilingual English–German studies in the sixth grade at all schools. Teaching young people to speak German is crucial to our strategy for strengthening French–German relations, in keeping with the solemn undertakings made by General de Gaulle in 1963.

After primary and secondary school, the next front must focus on providing career guidance, before and after high school matriculation. This is all the more urgent, in my view, because it does not appear to be of concern to those currently in charge of the educational system. Today, about 100,000 young people exit our system without a qualification or vocational training. Besides, although 80 per cent of the age group reach the final year of high school, there are many who are lost later in university courses that are inappropriate and which they abandon. This is a waste for them and for society.

Profound injustices are created in this system. Students from comfortable backgrounds who achieve good results at school go on to special classes preparing them for the elite institutions of higher education, or enter competitive high-level job-entry programs. Not to mention the increasing number of young people who go abroad to attend a British, Australian, American, or European university. On the other hand, when young people receive no guidance, they often find themselves on a university track by default, when a program aimed at gaining employment or another subject would have been suited them better.

We must therefore radically improve career guidance, beginning with middle schools.

The changes we need to make here should not be based on what the current system sees as satisfactory or worthwhile. Instead, they need to take into account the potential of every French student. They must be fully informed so that they can make their own choices. It is in this spirit that I recommend institutions' student performance for the three prior years be made public, to guide students registering for a university or vocational-training track.

People need to know how many students complete their studies and how many have found employment or are pursuing further studies. Transparency, and better-informed students and families, are the only ways to return to a fair balance in the system.

Vocational training should be considered an asset in its own right in our educational system. It relates first and foremost to better career guidance. If vocational alternatives are not progressing as they should, it is because they are disregarded or even opposed by the system. Another reason is that our companies remain insufficiently involved in training. Let's make things more straightforward. The state should define the programs and the framework of vocational training, and the management of these tracks should be decentralized to the regions.

Finally—universities. They are teeming with successes and world-firsts. We have been honored with Nobel Prizes and with prestigious awards in numerous disciplines. All over France there have also been innovations on the ground, and this reflects energy and a desire to forge ahead. There is also a certain pride in being a university student.

By shining a light on all these successes, we will give our students and researchers, French and foreign, a taste for the French university. This is essential for our social cohesion—and for our economy.

The challenges our universities face are not, however, to be taken lightly. The number of students has rocketed, and this trend will continue. Since 1960, the number of staff in institutions of higher learning has multiplied by eight. International competition has intensified, and this too will continue. Asia is now an actor in its own right, from Japan to China and elsewhere. Today, universities in Paris are not simply competing with one another: their competitors now include the *École polytechnique fédérale de Lausanne* in Switzerland, or the London School of Economics in the United Kingdom. Thanks to the digital revolution, it is now possible to follow a course at MIT (the Massachusetts Institute of Technology in Boston) from Paris, without registering, without being a student, and at a very low cost.

The knowledge market is gradually being thrown wide open. Entire sections of the economy are being overturned. Millions of jobs are being transformed—in manufacturing, in banking, and in the insurance industry. It is worth noting that the rate of unemployment that we are experiencing also reflects our difficulty in seizing these new economic opportunities. We will only remain among the leading economies of the world if our universities adapt and their instruction evolves.

In today's context, if we want to succeed, we must allow our universities greater pedagogical independence, and give them more resources. We must protect disadvantaged students with meaningful state aid. We must permit universities to apply higher charges to the most affluent, ensure that institutions have the means to attract the best educators, and open university libraries in the evenings and on weekends to meet students' needs, as is done in a number of other countries, notably in the United States. Let us get rid of outmoded dogma. Its first victims are our youth. Our only duty is to enable our students to succeed.

———

The way to achieve this is, of course, through our teachers. For me, the problem docs not lie in an alleged "recruitment crisis". The number of candidates for the teaching profession has never been so high. It lies instead in the functioning of our education system, specifically in the way in which teachers' transfers are technocratically co-managed by the administration and the national trade unions.

Rigid and obscure rules on transfers have created an intolerable situation, both for the teachers concerned and for the children from disadvantaged areas such as Seine-Saint-Denis, in the Paris suburbs: teachers appointed there are too young, inexperienced, and insufficient in number.

The number of rules and regulations is endlessly expanding, in particular the infamous "circulars". Support schemes, experiments, assessments, and skills–sharing across disciplines all need to be improved. On the one hand, the ministry can't resist telling their public officials — more than a million in number — in the greatest detail what they need to do. On the other hand, conservative voices protest at the mere mention of the word "independence", interpreting it as the collapse of the equality so beloved of the French Republic. We must, as a matter of urgency, help people to understand that uniformity is unrelated to equality: to act in the same way towards everyone is guaranteed to ensure that only a small minority do well. On the contrary, we must do more for those who have less.

How can we honestly believe that a primary school

in a priority educational zone, where 60 per cent of the children cannot read or write in fifth grade, might be able to meet the same challenges as a school in a more affluent neighborhood? Should the same level of investment be made in these schools on the pretext of our passion for equality? It is my conviction that we should give the former greater resources and far more autonomy. These schools should be allowed to try what has never been attempted: to attract the best instructors by paying them better salaries and also increasing the number of teaching hours. To support real equality, we need to give more to those who have the greatest need.

In practice, everything depends on the trust we place in the actors on the ground. They are in the best position to seek out, organize, and finance the most exciting innovations. I am thinking, in particular, of new "e-learning" methods, which would enable students who are not able to read after first grade, but go on to second grade in elementary school, to catch up.

In the same spirit, educational institutions must capitalize on the autonomy granted them, and this will serve as a new model for the reorganization of the system. The natural corollary of this shift is that an independent and authoritative body will be created to evaluate such establishments, based on clear, common goals. This means that instructors will be able to introduce more initiatives on the ground, to test and adapt methods based on student needs, with their sole aim being a better learning experience. I favor the release of significant resources for teams of instructors wishing to form groups and try out new ideas. Much trust will be placed in their work, but they will obviously be expected to report their results. Nothing would prevent them offering to create radically innovative educational entities—whether primary or middle schools, or high schools.

We will succeed in this revolution if we rediscover the essence of our commitment to the Republic, and if we once more place the teaching profession at its heart. My own career has made me tangibly aware of the extent to which instruction and the passing on of knowledge are the fundamental challenges. Sadly, something has broken down in the contract between the nation and its teachers. It is a fracture that the Right has allowed to expand, and that the Left was unable to repair. The Left even believed that, in some circumstances, it could exploit that situation, and the French people, particularly the disadvantaged, were fully conscious of this. It is a moral error that needs to be put right.

If we fail to take into account the moral well-being of our teachers, we will achieve nothing. I mean those young teachers thrown in at the deep end in difficult zones, inexperienced teachers confronted with problems of discipline, and holders of doctorates waiting long years to be appointed to the first level of university staff and then decades more to be appointed as professors.

Further problems concern burdensome administrative tasks, deteriorating relations with parents, financial remuneration that is not reviewed often enough, and teachers being told to work harder to earn the same amount or even less.

Very often, and we must not shy away from saying this, teachers' discontent does not find its origins in society, but in the teaching world itself. The issues include an omnipresent administration; a complicated system of co-management; and institutions being run in a way that blurs the line between independence and compliance with rules handed down from on high. Their discontent is further exacerbated by continual changes in the curriculum, and by relying on ministry software to decide students' fate, rather than on the instructors who know them so much better.

So, yes, it is possible to bring about a revolution in our schools—by working alongside them, hand in hand.

CHAPTER NINE

Making a living

I do not believe that it is the role of politics to promise happiness. The French people are not that easily taken in. They know very well that politics cannot achieve everything, that politics does not have the means to solve all problems, to govern everything, or to make everything better. Rather than focusing on a notional pursuit of happiness, it is my conviction that politics must deploy a framework that will enable every man and woman to find their way, to become masters of their own destiny and to exercise their freedom—to be able to choose how they live their lives. It is with this promise of emancipation that politics must engage. However, in order to be able to choose how we live our lives, we first need to be able to make a living.

Because it is by working that we can earn a living, educate our children, enjoy life, acquire knowledge, and forge ties with others. It is work, too, that enables us to rise above our situation and to carve out a place for ourselves in society. I therefore cannot believe those who predict the "end of work".

The de facto reservation of jobs for the most productive, writing off one section of the population as economically "useless", has always seemed to me to be a resounding failure to fulfill the finest promise made by the Republic—the emancipation of one and all. That is why I am convinced that the fight against unemployment must remain our priority. And the example set by our partners who have achieved success, starting with Germany, shows that this is not fated to be a losing battle. Solutions exist, but we need courage to apply them.

I do not believe that "full employment" alone will be enough to restore confidence in the nation. Examples from the United Kingdom or the United States, where that goal was reached, bear witness: Brexit and the accession to power of Donald Trump are symptoms of the distress that societies undergo when they give up on equality.

We need to provide jobs for all, and ensure that each job comes with proper remuneration and prospects. Where do we stand today regarding this promise?

Our employment market is unhealthy at all levels. A high rate of unemployment has become entrenched. It impacts one person in ten of working age, one young person in four, and, in certain problematic districts, one person in two. Entire swathes of the country have been excluded from employment, which feeds into feelings of despair and anger in those who live there, and creates both a fertile breeding ground for Islamic radicalization and votes in favor of the National Front.

These concerns pervade society. From childhood, we are beleaguered by the wrong choices that we make—in our studies, our jobs, or the industry we work in—and any of these factors can derail us. Even those who are employed are not necessarily secure. Alongside those who hold secure permanent contracts, there are millions of people condemned to constant instability: 70 per cent of employees are hired under short-term contracts—of less than one month in duration—and are then often rehired by the same company. There are also all those who can no longer manage to make ends meet, such as the vast numbers of farmworkers or those reduced to part-time work—who are, for the most part, women.

Our country needs rules that enable everyone to make a living. Unfortunately, our current regulations, conceived at the end of the Second World War, fail to meet contemporary challenges.

They favor "insiders", those who have jobs and better protection than others, at the expense of "outsiders"—the youngest, the least qualified, the most vulnerable. This is what has made our social model both unjust and inefficient: it favors rules, and paralyzes social mobility.

I want, first of all, to ensure that everyone can find a place in the job market, whatever their scholastic trajectory. Today, there are two million young people without employment or qualifications, as well as millions of unqualified or barely qualified workers.

We must give these people access to jobs without compromising on the importance of obtaining qualifications. So we should make apprenticeship systematic for all vocational training up to high-school certificate level, focus resources on lower-level qualifications, and place more emphasis on specific occupational sectors to allow people to train for the jobs they have chosen to go into.

In many sectors, including the construction industry, qualifications are essential, and we must recognize their importance. However, they sometimes exclude the most vulnerable and the least qualified by preventing them from setting up their own business and becoming self-employed. Whereas, in fact, for some people it is easier to find a customer than an employer. For anyone living in Stains in the Paris suburbs or Villeurbanne on the outskirts of Lyon, it is far easier to set up on one's own and look for customers than to get a job interview. To prevent such people from creating their own company by establishing minimum qualification requirements is to condemn them, whether young or not so young, to unemployment.

In this regard, I think of Michel, a man I met in Colmar. At fifty years of age, after spending thirty years in a car-body shop without having a vocational qualification (the Certificate of Professional Aptitude), he could no longer find work. He was too old. And on top of that, he was prohibited from establishing his own company! Did he have the means, or even the time, to obtain the required Certificate? No. As a result, he was condemned to long-term unemployment.

The primary obstacle preventing young people, particularly the less qualified, from finding employment is the cost of labor. I do not believe that the creation of a minimum wage for young people is the best way to address the problem, which must be confronted rationally. This is why apprenticeships need to be supported. Apprentices receive a lower salary, but benefit from qualifying training that will later enable them to be integrated into the workforce. For this reason, I hope to make the requirements for apprenticeship more flexible, by relaxing governance of the system and allowing those in the relevant occupational sectors to have more say in defining training programs.

Apart from the cost of labor already mentioned, there are costs involved in dismissing an employee. Cases brought before labor-relations boards are currently protracted, complex, and lack transparency. Large companies that have the staying power to handle the system, and the battery of lawyers needed to unravel its complexity, do not suffer. It is the salaried employees with little training who, after losing their jobs and waiting for months, sometimes years, to reach the outcome of the proceedings and to be paid compensation, pay the price. Victims also include small-business owners with one or two employees who, while waiting for a court judgment, refrain from hiring more workers. This is why I have been fighting to reform labor-relations boards, and will continue to do so. It is another reason why I will implement maximum and minimum thresholds for damages awarded in such situations.

At the same time, we must protect the standard of living of our workforce. This goes beyond the question of purchasing power. It is a matter of dignity and respect. How can we accept the way in which large numbers of farmers now have to live? How can we accept the fact that so many employees feel that they are very poorly paid for their work? I believe that promises of uncontrolled salary increases across the board made from on high are harmful: they penalize our companies, and ultimately the employees, and they generate unemployment.

We have a crucial battle ahead to increase purchasing power. It is truly unacceptable that the social protections that benefit everyone are based primarily on income from employment. This is one of the reasons why so many of our compatriots are surprised to see companies complaining of the high "cost of labor" when they themselves have the feeling that they are being inadequately remunerated for their efforts.

This is why I am proposing to reduce employee contributions and those paid by the self-employed. This will enable us to markedly raise net salaries, without adding to labor costs, harming competitiveness, or endangering jobs. We will finance this measure in such a way that workers will be the winners.

Regarding the most disadvantaged, benefit reforms will also be necessary. They should be withdrawn less rapidly when the employee returns to work—our objective should be to encourage a return to the labor market and to support the income of the poorest. Instead, we are doing the exact opposite!

———

Fighting for everyone to be able to make a living also enables economic actors to contend with changes that the legislator cannot always foresee. It is unthinkable that we could govern agriculture, luxury goods, artisanal products, and communications in the same way. Nevertheless, in labor matters, we continue to administer everything through legislation.

More than ever, we need to be agile and flexible at all levels: that means reorganizing our Labor Code.

To succeed in a knowledge economy driven by speed and innovation, organizations must be able to adapt constantly. If heads of companies fear that this may not be possible, they will shy away from taking on employees—or will not take on enough of them. To offer employees the best possible social contract, in accordance with the economic climate and the requirements of the sector, more possibilities for negotiation and dialogue must be opened up.

Sadly, the rules that we have in this regard in France are too numerous and too inflexible, and, because they are stipulated by the law, they cut across all types of companies and all types of business sectors, indiscriminately. This makes no sense.

We have seen the consequences of such an approach with the 35-hour week. Will those who today argue that we should move from a 35-hour week to a 39-hour week explain to the French people that they will have to work four more hours without being properly paid? That, too, will make no sense. For certain companies, the 35-hour week meets their needs perfectly. For others, it is not the case: they need management and labor to be willing to work together as partners—for longer hours (for example, to fill orders), or for fewer hours (for example, to avoid dismissals).

In situations where the law permits it, notably in large vehicle or shipbuilding companies, slightly longer working weeks have enabled thousands of jobs to be saved. The same trade unions that were blocking negotiations at national level, and were ideologically opposed to this type of reform, then approved an agreement at the company level. As minister, I went to Saint-Nazaire to sign orders for the construction of a new liner, where eighteen months earlier the company was about to close. It survived, thanks to the collective intelligence of the management and employees, who together were able to reach an agreement providing for partial unemployment for many months. Thanks to that agreement and with the support of the state as a shareholder, it proved possible to save the company and for it to rapidly resume activity when the first new orders were received. It now has advance orders for more than ten years, which is unprecedented. This just shows that nothing is ever pre-ordained.

By the same token, a reform that takes into account how onerous a job is, even if such a reform is a good thing in principle, cannot be applied across the board in the same manner. For a large automobile group, the reform does not create a problem, and represents real progress for employees. For a very small construction company or a bakery, it is almost impossible to implement. It will only serve to complicate life for business owners, and will weigh heavily on their ability to take on staff.

We therefore have to abandon the idea that the law can make provision for all eventualities—for everyone, in every situation.

I favor a profound change in the way in which our labor laws are constructed—so that the law is able to accommodate exceptions, through bargaining by business-sector and individual-company agreements passed by majority decision, on any matter.

Let us acknowledge that the Labor Code should define the overarching principles on which we are not willing to compromise, such as gender equality, working hours, and minimum salary. And then let us entrust to industry-level collective bargaining, and, in the alternative, specific company bargaining, the responsibility for ensuring a fair balance and appropriate protection.

In this way, we will be able to simplify matters at a grassroots level, while putting our faith in the intelligence of the parties involved. Today, we recognize that citizens can express themselves legitimately on any subject by using their vote. Why should we think that they might not be qualified to decide on matters that concern their daily lives?

I do not believe for a moment that we can create tomorrow's prosperity by unilaterally reducing the rights of all employees. But nor do I believe that we can succeed in a globalized world with rules that are inflexible and sometimes totally inappropriate.

I am not unaware of the fears that this approach might engender. In the French system, contrary to those of Germany and Scandinavia, there has been little familiarity with this method of discussion, negotiation, and compromise. Our trade unions are sometimes too weak; sometimes, not sufficiently representative. Nevertheless, social dialogue is not a luxury. It is at the heart of the approach that I am proposing. Not the social dialogue practiced at a national level in recent years, but rather a pragmatic dialogue, at the level of the business sector and the company. This requires us to draw the conclusion that we must reaffirm the legitimacy of trade unions, and provide them with negotiating tools. To support this development, we will therefore introduce an uncomplicated financing mechanism through which employees can direct resources made available by their company toward the trade union of their choice.

Finally, if we want everyone to be able to make a living in an innovation economy, people should have access to high-quality training throughout their lives.

Companies and even entire business sectors are being dismantled at ever-increasing speed: this should not be tantamount to condemning those employed there either to unemployment or to insecurity. Because, at the same time, new professions, new opportunities, and new jobs are constantly becoming available—and we must allow everyone, whatever their career path, to take advantage of them. It is no longer practicable to know at the age of twenty what we will do at the age of fifty. In order for work to provide a means of emancipation, we must propose a revised approach to continuing education. People can no longer be trained once, at the age of twenty, for their entire lives.

We cannot promise job security in a world that is subject to constant change—a world where technological developments are making some occupations obsolete while creating others. We cannot promise that every job will always be interesting and productive, because that was never the case. Those who make this claim are the hypocrites from whom we have inherited today's society.

However, there are two things that we can guarantee: people will be able to move from one occupation to another, and they will be protected if they lose their employment. For it is at times of great change that we owe the most to solidarity—to enable us to turn the corner.

Workers spend less and less of their careers in the same company or in the same business sector. We will therefore have an increasing need for time during our lives to acquire new qualifications.

Continuing education is not designed for that. In France, more than thirty billion euros are spent annually on vocational training. Nevertheless, here too it is the most vulnerable who have the greatest difficulty in gaining access to training. Our system is too complicated.

To obtain funding for training, a person may not know whether to contact a benefit agency, a regional authority, or the National Employment Agency. All the steps required can take up to a year, and many abandon the process before they complete it. In addition, the service rendered is not always up to standard. And it is principally reserved for those who have stable employment and are already well trained.

Here, too, we must initiate a real revolution—by offering everyone a program of personalized support, and an evaluation of professional and personal competencies as well as aptitudes and motivations, matched on the side of beneficiaries by a serious commitment and regular attendance. We then have to offer a large assortment of options, ranging from a short training course of a few weeks to master a key technique, to a longer course of a year or two—at a university, for example—for those aiming to make a complete career change.

To achieve this, the system will need to be more transparent, equipped with an effective method of assessment and the publication of results, in terms of the numbers who return to work and their salary advancement. Most importantly, all workers must be able to benefit from training resources and have direct contact with training providers, without go-betweens.

Such training must also be available to employees who have a position, but who suffer from a lack of prospects and from working conditions that have deteriorated. That is why we must make rights to unemployment insurance available to support training and retraining efforts for those who resign from their jobs. In this respect, unemployment insurance will change its nature. It will no longer be a question of insurance as such, but rather a way for career change and training to be financed by the authorities—the establishment of a universal right to professional mobility.

Unemployment insurance must also be accessible equally to the self-employed, to small-business owners, and to artisans, especially at a time when the difference between salaried employees and the self-employed is becoming blurred in the new service economy. The self-employed are often more exposed to risks and disruptions in their business. They are, at the same time, the least protected by our system. This is a cruel paradox that we must absolutely reject.

On the other hand, I am firmly against the debate launched by a number of political leaders regarding a sliding-scale approach to unemployment benefits: removing so many euros or so many months from existing entitlements. By focusing the argument this way, they imply that changes are irrelevant, that professional mobility will be achieved by itself, and that unemployment is more or less the fault of the unemployed. I believe, on the contrary, that massive public investment is necessary—but that it should be earmarked to serve training and qualifications, on condition that all parties involved assume responsibility for monitoring regular attendance and for the assessment of vocational training.

This revolution does not, however, imply a move to statism. The state must finance this training—as it already does, but without really making decisions—and guarantee that it functions properly. However, it should largely delegate skills assessment to private service-providers, as it has begun doing already. It should delegate training programs to regional authorities, professional associations, universities, schools, and vocational-training centers. The state will be in charge of evaluating them. In return, we will step up monitoring and requirements for job-seeking and training, so as to ensure the proper use of these funds. What I want is a system that is exacting with regard to rights and obligations. The equation is clear: after a certain period of unemployment, whoever has not completed training will not receive benefits. Nor will benefits be payable to anyone who has completed training and does not accept a reasonable offer of employment. This is the only way of ensuring that the money is spent fairly and effectively, and it will leverage significant savings.

However, when choosing how we are going to live, making a living is not enough. That promise cannot stand on its own. It must be supported by a complete revision of our social-protection system, emanating from a basic idea: doing more for those who have less.

CHAPTER TEN

Doing more for those
who have less

In a world where everything is changing so quickly, the French people need to take more risks and to innovate. That is the essence of the training revolution I outlined in the last chapter. However, in practice, such changes also create new inequalities. On the one hand, some of our compatriots are taking full advantage of the fact that our country is going global. They have received good training, and possess significant financial and cultural capital. On the other, we have more disadvantaged and more vulnerable citizens. Their fate is tied to the prevailing economic climate, and they are the first victims of heightened competition and technological transformations, lack of job security and unemployment, health problems, and the withdrawal of public services.

Some of these disparities can provide insights into

why our country is so deeply attached to equality. This conviction distinguishes us from other Western societies, particularly those in the English-speaking world. We are not willing to sacrifice everything in a race for economic growth, or on the altar of individualism. We seek a special kind of freedom — autonomy and independence underpinned by solidarity.

I am a strong believer in a society that provides choices — a society freed of any obstacles, and released from obsolete structural frameworks — in which all individuals can decide how to live their own lives. However, without solidarity, such a society would degenerate into separatism, exclusion, and violence. The freedom to make one's own life choices would be reserved for the strongest and not for the weakest.

We must therefore invent new means of protection and new ways of providing security. Fundamentally, we need to forge a response to the new inequalities.

For me, such a response comes from a basic awareness that uniformity — of rights, access, rules, aid schemes, and so on — no longer means equality. Quite the opposite. The challenge is no longer to offer everyone the same thing, but to provide each and every person with what they need. This is not the end of solidarity, but, on the contrary, its reinvigoration. When people's backgrounds and positions are more and more diverse, it is essential to move away from a uniform approach. If we fail to do this, public intervention will perpetuate and even exacerbate inequalities where it ought to correct them.

This requires a radical change in the role of the state. It must become a true "social investor" that sees individuals not as what they are, but as what they can become and what they can contribute to the public good.

So the state must not limit itself to providing a safety net — this is, of course, the least it should do. It needs to enable each and every person, wherever they are, to express all their talents and all their human qualities. This is true for the poorest, towards whom we must not only demonstrate financial solidarity, but furnish a genuine place in our society. It also applies to those who are the victims of ethnic or religious discrimination. Proclaiming rights is not enough. We must fight unstintingly for them to be upheld.

Here, a different method is needed. The state must place the accent on intervention before the fact, which is less costly and more effective. This is particularly evident in healthcare, where an ambitious prevention policy is essential.

Lastly, rights need to be extended to all citizens — particularly in relation to unemployment or pensions, so that special protection schemes do not create obstacles and injustices. The fact that some people have almost no protection and that, at the same time, others benefit from special regimes, is unacceptable. Every individual must have the same rights.

For almost nine million of our compatriots living below the poverty line who, once they have paid their day-to-day expenses, have less than 10 euros a day to live on, poverty is not a risk but a reality. And for the many French people who are constantly on the verge of a downward spiral into hardship, it is a daily concern.

As far as this question is concerned, the political class positions itself according to two predominant points of view, which have been entrenched for a very long time. According to the first view, shared by a number of politicians on the Right, most beneficiaries of social welfare benefits are scroungers. We therefore ought to make the lives of the poorest even more difficult and make them feel guilty about their situation. According to the second view, held by some of those on the Left, we could just pay out a few benefits—without focusing close attention on who receives them. I reject both approaches on the grounds that, once again, they lead to discord at the very heart of French society.

There is also another temptation, spanning both the Left and the Right, which relates to the "guaranteed minimum income". This would consist of paying everyone—without conditions relating to resources or any other eligibility requirement—an amount that ensures personal subsistence levels. I do see how the idea can be appealing, but I don't go along with it. First of all, for financial reasons. We would have to choose, on the one hand, between a low minimum income, which would in no way address the questions emanating from serious poverty and would even worsen matters for the deprived, and, on the other, a high minimum income that could only be engineered at the cost of significant tax pressure on the middle classes. But there is an even more fundamental reason. I believe in work as a value, as a means of emancipation, as a vector of social mobility. And I do not believe that some people are, by definition, destined to subsist on the fringes of society, with no other prospects than to spend the limited income allotted to them.

In other words, I believe that we owe solidarity, aid, and consideration to the most vulnerable. Solidarity obliges us first of all to enable the poorest to access the aid to which they are entitled. One-third of the people who could potentially benefit from the "Active Solidarity Income" scheme do not apply for it. Why? For some, because they don't know it exists. For others, because they choose not to put in an application.

Our duty to respect others means that we must recognize all of their qualities and enable them to find work in our society wherever possible. This takes different forms, depending on the person.

First of all, we have to be uncompromising with cheats — they are far from being in the majority, but they do exist. Because, quite apart from the financial cost that society has to bear as a result of fraudulent claims, these people undermine the very idea of solidarity that keeps us shoulder to shoulder, by feeding into accusations of scrounging and bringing suspicion upon all those who are fully entitled to receive benefits. Social-benefit fraud and tax fraud — the latter far exceeding the former in terms of extent — undermine the trust of many of our compatriots in government action. This requires strong measures to be taken.

We also need to provide diligent and individual support for those who are able to return to the world of work. In this regard, as in so many other areas, the know-how of organizations working on solidarity and social enterprise, which are at the forefront of social innovation outside urban centers, seems to me of vital importance. That know-how deserves to be propagated more widely. Here, too, an ambitious plan providing access to further qualifications, supported by the continuing education reforms that I have already discussed, would offer a real break with the past in view of the tentative measures that have been the norm in the last twenty years.

Lastly, we need to recognize—and understand—that some people are excluded from the labor market for very long periods and that it will be hard for them to ever find work again. They may be disabled, there may be things they cannot do, or they may have had a very challenging life trajectory. And yet they cannot be left by the wayside. We have a duty to offer them, as far as possible, work that is at the same time gratifying for them as individuals and useful for the community. In this way, they can find their place, recover their dignity, and get involved. For too long we have taken it for granted that giving money to people who can no longer make ends meet would settle everything. We owe them much more than this.

Formulating policies to combat poverty hand-in-hand with those affected would be a mark of respect, and a guarantee of the policies' future effectiveness.

Doing more for those who have less also means not tolerating discrimination—whether related to gender, ethnic origins, sexual preference, opinions, disability, or health issues. Discrimination is intolerable in all its forms, because it is an attack on who we are. Furthermore, discrimination has a high social and economic cost.

The first type of discrimination directly concerns half of the French population—women—every day of the week. Daily life in today's France is very different depending on whether one is a man or a woman. The labor market is an edifying example. Women are often obliged to work fewer hours: 78 per cent of part-time workers are women. They are paid less: in an equivalent job and working the same hours, a woman will earn 10 per cent less than a man. They also have fewer executive responsibilities: only three of the 40 largest listed French companies that form the CAC40 are headed by women. Only 30 per cent of start-ups are founded by women.

Worse still, and day in, day out, women alone have to endure a form of insecurity that men do not—a thousand-and-one situations on public transport, at work, and in the street that expose them to insidious and unacceptable forms of harassment. This was widely reported by the women we encountered during a public consultation organized in 2016 by *En Marche!* volunteers.

The second type of discrimination relates to ethnic origins. For a long time, we believed that anti-racism measures were enough to combat the injustice weighing upon all those who are not born with the right skin color, the right religion, or in the right place. Such mobilization against racism was highly prevalent in the 1980s. It represented a major, welcome change in awareness for French society, which had tended to see injustice solely in terms of social class. However, this approach, too, had its limits. It often proved to be excessively moralistic, and was inadequate to stop community tensions mounting. More importantly, it did nothing to improve the daily lives of ethnic and religious minorities, who were often alienated by this behavior. Condemning injustice is not enough. We need action.

Overt racism is intolerable — but discrimination is even more insidious, and can be even more destructive. We can take issue with insults and sarcasm. But what can be done in the face of job applications that are never answered, or promotions that are given to everyone else, but not to you? We feel helpless, powerless. We can do very little about this if we act alone. Recent studies have shown that a job candidate appearing to be a Muslim received a quarter of the replies received by a candidate who appeared to be a Catholic. Public authorities must increase the number of checks, and make them systematic and more stringent. Employers with unacceptable practices must realize that they will be identified and fined. The Republic must take a far stronger stand on this issue. I am convinced that we will make no progress as long as people do not feel directly concerned by the problem — in particular, all those who have never experienced discrimination.

Discrimination against women, or ethnic and religious minorities, or disabled persons must not obscure the full picture or the manifold forms of discrimination. The law lists more than twenty. We need to have more weapons in our legislative arsenal, and ensure that laws are enforced—and we must take aim at each and every instance of discrimination. In this area, the law has the potential to make a difference. As an example, it has enabled the proportion of women with seats on boards of directors and supervisory boards at CAC40 companies to be increased: between 2009 and 2015, the number of women increased threefold.

Nevertheless, the law is not enough to combat discrimination, so in parallel we need to develop proactive policies that will allow us to eradicate it. I want to make "testing" policies routine. There are some extremely effective methods such as sending out hundreds of résumés that are identical—apart from the small matter of gender, or ethnic or religious origin—to see whether some, groundlessly, receive fewer replies than others.

Doing more for those who have less, and thereby protecting the weakest, also includes disease prevention. Here, too, there is deep injustice. We often boast about having the best healthcare system in the world. Reality, however, is not so clear-cut. While we have some of the best researchers, hospitals, and healthcare professionals in the world, French healthcare does not provide such high-quality service as is commonly believed and, worse still, harbors severe inequalities.

People are often unaware that France has very mediocre success rates for all of the pathologies that require prevention—cancer, cirrhosis, and so on—and that the first to suffer from these diseases come from underprivileged backgrounds. Let's take just two examples out of thousands: farmers' children suffer 50 per cent more from tooth decay than do the children of executives, and obesity is three times higher in factory workers' children than in those of their managers.

In the light of all this, I do not believe that the solution lies in pitting hospitals against what are called community clinics. On the contrary, wherever possible we should foster complementarity and partnerships among them. Nor do I believe that we should only think about health in terms of budget size or the social security debt. The question is not whether consultation costs should be increased by two or three euros—or not. Once again, we are missing the point and overlooking the real problems.

The fundamental issues are elsewhere. We have to find other approaches to ensure that prevention becomes the cornerstone of our healthcare policy. To find ways and means for people to retain their dignity in old age and remain independent for as long as possible. To stop 73,000 of our compatriots dying every year from tobacco-related illnesses, and 50,000 others from alcohol abuse.

Here, too, we need a revolution—starting with placing

a priority on preventive consultations. This means that we need to release doctors from administrative tasks, and new support roles should be created so that they can hand over certain duties. It also means that we need to modernize our economic model. Charging per patient visit cannot continue to be the only way in which general practitioners are paid. New ways of contracting need to be available; for example, we could envisage fixed tariffs for sensitive groups such as the very young and the very old, leaving practitioners free to take them on or not.

I will also maintain a high level of solidarity in healthcare spending. We must move forward in a smart way. And not by making tiny tweaks each year solely to stay within budget. We need to think about reforms, not on a year-to-year basis, as the current healthcare funding approach prompts us to do, but to envision them in the long term. This is the only way to bring about fundamental reforms and to achieve a sustainable transformation of our system.

On that basis, we will be able to take on the much-needed revitalization of public hospitals. For many years now, they have been facing a serious lack of resources, of capacity, and of common sense. We can no longer ignore this crisis.

We need to separate practices from institutions. The transformation of our healthcare system cannot be managed by central government alone. Once again, I am convinced that we need to give more autonomy to healthcare actors on the ground, in particular at regional level. These are the people who know best the area's needs and the individual character of its people. This is exactly what I saw in Chamonix, where a health center was created to enable doctors to work more efficiently together, and to invest in infrastructure and in innovative methods such as telemedicine. Or a hospital in Sallanches, where a partnership with private practitioners was established to keep open an institution that had become too small, and to facilitate patients' speedy discharge in order to reduce costs and improve their care. Change will not be dictated from above. It will be driven at grassroots level.

Lastly, French citizens are not all equal when it comes to unemployment or pensions. Both our unemployment insurance and pension schemes are emblematic of a system that was built for a world where the worker—a man—spent his whole life at the same company. He paid his contributions for his pension and his healthcare, with little fear of being laid off, and without having to consider changing careers. He had no concerns about job insecurity or external competition.

Our system has, of course, been through many changes in the last few decades: we have had four sets of pension reforms since 2003 alone. Despite this, the system still benefits first and foremost those working at large companies, who are in good health, hired on stable contracts of employment, with a linear career path from first job to retirement. But these people are becoming rarer and rarer.

We can no longer accept cobbled-together solutions or the umpteenth discussion about a particular problem. We need to realize that the current system, which depends on each individual's employment status at their company, and is funded essentially by the workforce, no longer meets the needs of a society that has been suffering from mass unemployment for more than three decades. The focus of debate needs to move away from whether people should retire at 65 or at 62 years of age, or how many qualifying periods are needed to be eligible. Those questions do need to be addressed, of course, with regard to demographic trends, intergenerational fairness, and the financial robustness of the pensions system. The point is not to try to police the line between salaried workers and the self-employed in order to define who can pay into unemployment insurance and who cannot. The real questions that we need to ask ourselves are even more fundamental. How can we take effective action to ensure that no one is sidelined? How can we be sure that everyone can find a place in a society that is so profoundly different from the past?

As the world of work is becoming more and more compartmentalized into a multitude of positions, jobs, and contracts, and as career paths are less linear, our social security system is no longer able to level out inequalities, and in fact feeds into them.

How easy is it for people to understand their pension entitlements when they have worked, for example, first in the public sector, then in the private sector, and were then self-employed, moving from one pension fund to another and from one scheme to another? How can we explain to a farmer who has worked hard all his life that he will receive a negligible pension from the agricultural pension fund, and that his wife who was at his side, helping him every day of their lives, will have nothing? We are all familiar with the nightmare of calculating entitlements when a career has involved several moves. Unfairly, entitlements are very different, even for the same job, depending on one's contractual status. What social-mobility opportunities do we offer those on tenuous temporary contracts who do not benefit from the prospects they would have at a large company?

The principle for this essential transformation is thus clear: social protection must be forged around and for the individual, with the aim of mainstreaming entitlements and achieving transparency and equality. It is no longer workers, according to their contractual status or category, who need to be protected, but each and every one of us, whatever our situation at a given time, on an equal basis—as is the case now for health insurance.

I have already talked about the need to foster and safeguard career moves. Here I would like to highlight the new social-protection map that ensues. In order to encourage career mobility, the pensions system needs to be simpler and easier to understand. It is not acceptable that it should be so difficult to understand our entitlements, or that they should vary so much depending on our employment history. The various schemes should be merged over the next few years, to gradually create a universal pension scheme. Pensions should not, in the long term, depend on whether people are employed or self-employed, or are civil servants, but on what they actually do. And it is on this basis that the question of how long we should pay into a scheme must be assessed, rather than treating the issue indiscriminately across the board. This would be clearer for everyone, and would at the same time be fairer.

It no longer makes sense, in view of the high risk of unemployment, for our system to be based on such a narrow insurance mechanism. Today, only employed workers are insured. As I have said, mainstreaming and a thorough overhaul of the system are essential. We need a system based on solidarity—to which each person has to contribute, and from which each person can benefit. Such a system would therefore cover not only employed workers who are made redundant or resign from their jobs, but also the self-employed. The implication in terms of funding is that its basis needs to be tax and no longer social security contributions. Similarly, benefits will no longer come under an umbrella of insurance, but of measures fostering solidarity. As a result, the upper threshold for payments, now almost 7,000 euros per month—more than three times higher than the European Union average—will be lowered. There will also be an immediate outcome in terms of governance.

In view of the fact that insurance will no longer relate to one or other category of worker, since social protection will be financed less and less by contributions and more and more by tax, the state will need to take on responsibility for the strategic decisions that thus far have been delegated to social security agencies. Up to now, these organizations, representing both employees and employers, needed to reach agreement on all of the conditions relating to unemployment benefits, such as their amount, duration, and associated obligations on the part of the receiver. Despite this, it is the state that acts as guarantor for the unemployment benefit debt—without having any real say in the way in which the system is organized. It is for this reason that I believe that public authorities should take back responsibility for decisions relating to unemployment insurance. The authorities cannot continue to be the silent guarantors of a crumbling system, where the only option is to place curbs on it. They can no longer simply be the heralds of a compromise … which is never achieved.

Basically, I believe that the state must place the onus on social security agencies in collective-bargaining processes, the oversight of employer firms, and the provision of support for people during their working lives, and reduce these agencies' input in the management of the system. It is going to be a real battle. It is going to incur the wrath of all those who are comfortably ensconced in the system. But it will be a release for all those compatriots who are currently thwarted by it. So we must, of course, go ahead. It is among the most important items on our agenda that need addressing. There will be no place for dogma, though. No reason to put an end, out of principle, to the participation of social security agencies in governance initiatives, but rather to rebalance the current position. In the area of sickness benefit, for example, governance is balanced and satisfactory.

———

In the next years and decades, dependency will become more and more of an issue. First of all, because the French population as a whole is ageing: in 2050, one French citizen out of three will be over 60 years old, as against one in five only ten years ago. Next, because the first cohorts of the baby-boom generation will be 80 years old in 2025. A longer lifespan is great news for all of us. However, in order for that progress to be a truly positive step, we should aspire to the adage: "It's not the years in your life that count. It's the life in your years." This means that we must enable older people to live their lives to the full, to maintain bonds with others, to get involved when they want to, to travel around as they wish, to be independent for as long as they can, and to continue to make useful contributions to society. The challenge is to ensure that our older citizens can live longer, in good health, and retain their independence.

It's not enough to agree on the goal—we need to revise our approach to solidarity in order to address the need for integrated care that, by 2050, will probably generate higher levels of spending than on pensions. This issue concerns the whole of society—older people, of course, but also the millions of families and care workers who look after our senior citizens on a day-to-day basis. The difficulty is to address a new set of circumstances, which relate neither to pensions nor to sickness, and which are going to affect all of us, without exception, directly.

CHAPTER ELEVEN

Reconciling France in all its guises

The French dream has always been one of unification. From its base in Paris, the state has long sought to achieve uniformity, to provide the same services and to put in place the same infrastructure all over France. Nevertheless, for many years now, the continuing fragmentation of our country has been happening before our very eyes.

France, like the rest of the world, is facing the effects of "metropolization". Large cities are the real winners in the opening up of our society, and they offer higher-value jobs. Moreover, 50 per cent of global GDP is generated in only three hundred of the world's cities, and 50 per cent of French GDP is generated in fifteen of our conurbations, with Paris and the greater Paris region ranking at the top. On the other hand, the rest of France hosts 80 per cent of the most disadvantaged: those who are hit hard by factory closures, the withdrawal of public services, and limited access to the labor market and to cultural activities.

By making this point, I don't mean we have to stop cities expanding. On the contrary: they are an opportunity for our country, a source of development, business, employment, and influence.

So, in that case, should we give up on this dream of a homogenous France, where a single model is to be applied in each region? I believe so. Let's face facts: people's lives are not the same when they live in Lyon or in the Normandy port of Cherbourg, and living in the suburbs of Paris or on the banks of the Loire is not the same thing. Needs for infrastructure and services differ from one place to another. The time when Paris could make the same promises all over the country is past. We now need to make sure that each conurbation can drive the development of neighboring areas, and help to harmonize economic activity.

However, at the same time, we need to remember that each city has a grave responsibility to its region. Today, our flourishing cities can ensure that no rural area in France is condemned to a bleak future. Conurbations house 40 per cent of the population, as well as creating 70 per cent of private-sector jobs created. A key step in France's development, in my view, is taking advantage of the complementary nature of our largest cities and our newly extended administrative regions.

While being essential to our future, cities also have their dark side. They attract people, sometimes from afar, wishing to escape poverty, and tend to lead to social divides. On the one hand, there are affluent districts bustling with vitality, and, on the other hand, some boroughs are getting poorer every day and even turning into ghettos. Today, life in our cities is all too often lived in uncomfortable proximity, and we should be aware that tomorrow, if we do nothing, this could mutate into a face-off.

This is why I firmly believe that the first of the social measures we need to take is to reconfigure our towns and cities, and bring back diversity. It's easy to see how everything ties together: children don't have the same life opportunities when they live in a neighborhood where 80 per cent of the inhabitants don't speak French at home, in suburbs that are gradually withdrawing from the outside world, or when they attend school with others of the same ethnic origin who, like them, are falling behind in their studies.

Yes, today, in our biggest cities, the social divide is first and foremost a division among neighborhoods. It is this tear in the social fabric that we need to fight the hardest, by implementing urban-regeneration policies and building housing with one sole aim—to ensure that towns are once more a place where people meet and socialize.

This presupposes that policies will be implemented at the right level and on a broader scale: councils need to work together. This applies to all large cities. It is even more important in the wider Paris area, Ile-de-France, where the reforms of the Greater Paris project will not, in my opinion, be enough to address the urgent issues facing the largest region in France.

This kind of reconfiguration requires considerable resources—whereas, in recent years, the budget of the

National Agency for Urban Regeneration has been slashed by more than half. Investments need to be supplemented by partnerships with the private sector, and guided by public authorities at the local level. If we want to succeed in meeting the challenges of building new housing, creating new public spaces, and establishing networks, our businesses' financial resources and expertise will be fundamental.

Yes—if we want to bring back diversity to our cities and tackle the new challenges facing us, we need to build accommodation. Our housing policy is obsolete. It was conceived for the families of yesteryear and not for the French citizen of today. It was designed as part of a sedentary society with a certain balance between different regions and traditional family values. Clearly, the people of France no longer live their lives in the same way. They have to change location far more often, if only to follow a more erratic career pathway. So housing needs are skyrocketing. When a couple divorces and they share custody of the children, it is not one two-bedroomed house that is needed, but two two-bedroomed houses.

In the last few years, the portion of the household budget set aside for housing has risen sharply. Prices of existing housing stock have increased by 150 per cent in 20 years, whereas available income has only increased by 50 per cent. This price issue clouds the main difficulty—one of quantity. Supply is not sufficient to satisfy demand, especially in areas where housing availability is particularly low, such as the greater Paris area, the Côte d'Azur, and a few other large cities where people have a particularly hard time finding a home.

In these areas where housing is in such short supply, I want to build homes on a far larger scale and far more quickly. In order to do this, we need to be consistent. We cannot continue to make town-planning laws even more complex, to add more technical regulations, or extend official procedures so that they take even longer. We need to stop prevaricating about this. Either the absolute priority is to build more housing, or we want over-regulation to prevail. Trying to adopt both of these approaches at the same time means guaranteed failure all round. I intend to do everything I can to build homes where our citizens need them.

Next, we need unstinting determination. We cannot accept elected representatives failing to fulfill their duty simply in order to preserve local political arrangements or high property prices. Construction plans for the greater Paris region show that most new-builds are concentrated in four or five municipalities, which exhibit almost identical features to those municipalities where no new homes are being built at all. The problem, then, is a political one. In those cities where the problem is most acute, the state must put in place special procedures to free up land, accelerate urban-planning processes, and enable the tens of thousands of additional homes required every year to be built without delay.

This targeted building initiative is the only effective way to meet demand for housing in cities and to bring down prices. In turn, this will enable the massive sums of state aid granted in the last few years to be reduced. Because, in fact, by attempting to help people with their household budgets without addressing the construction issue, we have fueled spiraling prices.

Surrounding the part of France that consists of cities and conurbations is another part—often referred to as the "periphery". There, people travel around, each in their own cars, which causes a problem from an ecological point of view, and also makes residents' lives more difficult as journeys between home and work take longer and longer, and the roads get busier and busier.

This "peripheral" France is often lacking in basic public infrastructure, transport links, child-care facilities, and cultural centers. Living conditions there can be of very low quality. We all know the problems of certain very run-down residential areas, and areas where homes are juxtaposed against warehouses and small-business units. That facet of France is suspicious of our society, rejects the system, and is gradually being attracted by extremism. That facet needs public and private investment in regeneration, and far more inter-municipal cooperation—in order to build a social fabric that can bring together the town and the green belt on the boundaries of conurbations in a harmonious and attractive way.

In parallel, we need to consolidate the dynamics of medium-sized towns—there are around one hundred of them—which underpin our country and its economy. In particular, their town centers. We know that, due to a lack of urban-planning foresight on a proper scale for commercial developments, permission was given for inappropriately large shopping malls to be built on the outskirts of these towns. The heart is now being ripped out of them as the shops and restaurants leave, one after another. The urban fabric is gradually deteriorating and giving rise to other major problems. These hubs should, on the contrary, constitute the vanguard of economic development, with small and medium enterprises providing jobs for the whole area. These "towns as centers" should therefore be protected.

As in the larger cities, some of these towns are faced with the problems of underprivileged districts. Here, too, we need to foster true diversity.

I have spoken about the fact that France has much to gain from its largest cities. However, not all of our conurbations have the same dynamics. Some regions with a historical industrial tradition have been experiencing a slump for many years, because the factories that were their flagships have progressively become obsolete.

We know that at the height of the financial crisis, some areas in the north-east of France lost up to 10 per cent of their jobs in only two years. Sadly, this decline has continued. It has dramatic consequences: higher and higher rates of unemployment, and young people who leave their region because they think there is no future there for them—and this makes things still worse. The situation is even more serious for workers who, having purchased a home and taken on a high level of debt, are no longer able to leave due to the collapse in house prices. Unless they surrender to losing everything.

In these regions, the inhabitants feel as if life has come to a complete standstill. Is it surprising that they have lost all hope?

In order to breathe life into these regions, the state needs to bear the brunt of the effort needed. Not by trying to perpetuate a now-outdated industry, whatever the cost, but by fostering a new growth strategy that is more in line with today's economy. This needs to be based on knowledge and know-how. University towns, in particular, must be supported to play a decisive role in training. This will have a knock-on effect throughout the territory. Start-ups need to be fostered, and—through innovation, a quest for quality, and the introduction of new processes—a number of traditional industrial sectors could be revived. None of them are truly condemned if we can find a way to position them in a modern context.

A great example of this can be seen in Besançon. When the company LIP closed in the early 1970s, it was the result of a lack of investment and a failure to anticipate changes in the clock industry, which formed the bedrock of this region. It was swept aside by the arrival of quartz technology. Today, there are more jobs in industry in Besançon than in the past. How did this happen? The municipal authorities, the province, the government, and the business community all invested in workers' skills and in innovation. The clock-making skills to be found there, involving a high level of precision, meant that hundreds of small and medium enterprises could be set up and then expand in this region. Innovation was nurtured by state-owned scientific institutes and private stakeholders, and turned that town into the capital of precision microtechnology.

This is how we need to conceive of economic development. And it explains why, in the field of industrial policy, I have never sought to defend, no matter the cost, companies lagging behind the times, but have instead sought to stimulate start-ups, or to use new technologies as a way to revive older firms. It is not jobs that we need to protect; it is the people in those jobs. We must therefore enable companies to transfer staff. Also, their employees should be able to benefit from continuing education programs. This is how they will be able to tackle, in the best possible circumstances, the great transformation that is under way.

Finally, I would like to talk about a last facet of France, which now feels so far removed from the expanding cities: rural France. Or rather: rural life. Is this feeling of abandonment inevitable? I don't believe so.

First, we have the question of the countryside as a life choice. More and more French people are moving to towns and cities. But they also love nature. For them, rural areas are highly attractive. They go there on vacation, and for the weekend. They restore farms and buildings in the centers of hamlets and villages that had previously been deserted.

Next, I believe that we have an opportunity to develop a productive economy in rural France. That economy may be first and foremost a residential one, based on the renovation of buildings, on tourism, and on the promotion of high-quality local products. Subsequently, in the longer term, it could take advantage of developments in new technologies that take distance out of the equation. Services such as call centers or digital outreach should be developed there. Industry may also relocate to rural areas, supported by innovation, as I have seen at the global fruit-processing company Andros, which is headquartered in south-west France.

These abandoned territories must become testing grounds for innovation. It is important to understand that "across the board" rules generated by the state and accompanied by over-cautiousness are the enemy of rural development—for the countryside is not fighting on a level playing field. Rural territories need to be able to take risks, to try things out, to experiment.

In the dozen-or-so rural provinces that are seeing their population fall every year, I would like to see a fresh approach applied. They have waited too long. It is here that the older generation and the farmers are reaching the end of their tether—they feel abandoned. And this is even more serious for France as a whole, because these territories form the very backbone and identity of our country. If they slip away, it will be our undoing.

Regarding transport infrastructure, each of these places—from Guéret to Mende, including Foix, Gap, and Aurillac—should have at least one fast transport link to a town or city, and to the places of business that are essential to their development. This requisite infrastructure must be built within five years. As for mobile networks and fiber optics, the state must intervene swiftly if operators fail to comply with their undertakings. Concerning healthcare, practical measures—such as locating health centers near existing hospitals, or creating groups of health practitioners—must be accelerated. As to energy, we need to adopt special initiatives to accelerate the creation of biogas plants and wind farms.

On the matter of public services, we need to ensure that schools are maintained everywhere, and to go even further with the creation of multi-service centers, such as those launched in recent years housed within post offices. Lastly, we must support farmers both with regard to their production and to land management. This will require a package of measures relating to agricultural land, inheritance, and protection against climate issues. In rural areas, the fight for our farmers, as I have already said, becomes an even more crucial one. Farmers are the women and men who form the bedrock of our landscape, of our country, who are the guardians of our land. And when despair pervades those fields, a part of our collective morale is lost. By reorganizing supply chains, we must reinstate stable and fair prices to enable them to make a living and to invest in the future.

Adapting public policies to local realities is therefore essential for the territories of mainland France. This must also apply to our overseas territories. We know how diverse they are, of course, in terms of history and geographical features, but also in their institutions. These regions include Martinique, Guadeloupe, Guiana, Réunion Island, Mayotte, and New Caledonia, as well as Saint Pierre and Miquelon, Saint-Barthélemy, Saint Martin, Wallis and Futuna, and French Polynesia. We are also aware of certain features that are common to them all: a rate of unemployment that is higher than the national average, particularly among young people; a high cost of living, even though wages are lower, with greater poverty as a result; a low quality of life; and inadequate infrastructure, despite the investments made after the Second World War.

Talking about equality is of no help in making regulations intelligible when you are 8,000 km or 10,000 km away from mainland France, when you are on an island with a very small and restricted market, and when you are surrounded by countries with low or very low wages, far from the Eurozone and its rules. I want these territories to have rules that enable them to innovate and, amongst other things, to be treated as fully fledged overseas entities, with a social security and tax regime that addresses their constraints, and a dynamic policy with incentives for private investment in innovative fields such as biodiversity or marine technology. These territories don't want handouts from mainland France. They want fair treatment so that they, too, can succeed, from their own base, within the Republic of France.

As France is one and indivisible, and at the same time so diverse, we must move away from a philosophy of uniformity and standardization, and towards differentiation and proactive policies. This is the key if we want to ensure that our country remains united.

This same vision for territorial diversity brings me to a new administrative and political structure for France. The state must decentralize, refocus, forge new partnerships across all levels of local and regional government, and develop policies that are appropriate for the different areas. Within the context of the recently formed larger administrative regions, it would be natural to create a relationship between regions and conurbations. In practice, I think that the conurbations could more often than not absorb the *départements* in their area.

In rural territories, municipal authorities will not be able to take on the responsibility for development: given these towns' smaller size, some administrative roles could be transferred to the *départements*. For some of the smallest, it might be necessary to group them together.

As a general rule, it is vital to re-establish solidarity among the different territories.

Here, dyed-in-the-wool quarrels need to be transcended. The question should not be whether one is for or against the concept of the "*département*". In areas where there are strong urban centers and powerful cities, I cannot see the relevance of a provincial level of government. Ile-de-France (Greater Paris) is a case in point. However, in primarily rural areas the *département* needs to be the very driver of territorial development.

I believe, first and foremost, that the territory should be structured based on proposals from the grassroots level. Here we might cite the recent initiatives aimed at merging the two *départements* in the former Alsace region, or creating a Brittany Assembly as the single regional authority there. One might also refer to the Rhône *département* and the city of Lyon. The different parts of our country have ideas about how to better share responsibilities and make savings. We need to ensure that we listen to them and hear what they are saying.

I know that I am breaking some taboos here. But it is in this way that we will be able to reduce public spending. Not through a policy of whittling budgets down indiscriminately across the board, but with a policy that gives rise to a win-win situation for every single area of France.

In this sphere, as in many others, I want France to belong to the stakeholders on the ground.

CHAPTER TWELVE

Caring for France

At a time when our country is having to live with heightened risk, terrorist violence, and the uncertainties of the modern world, it is very tempting to simply assert authority, make a show of strength, and reiterate our principles. Some people would like us to believe that declarations of authority can suffice in and of themselves to keep control of the country. They think that the issuing of bans and the maintaining of public order will do the rest, without any further plan of action. Others hold that France's identity is frozen, blinkered, and clinging to an imaginary and non-existent golden age.

Far from it. In the face of these serious issues, our country has only one choice — to stand shoulder to shoulder, united by a common will. We must demonstrate a firmness of purpose that provides impetus, and marks out borders that have a dual function — to bring us together and at the same time give meaning to matters that are beyond our understanding. France, then, is made up of people who care.

France does not reinvent itself every day from scratch. Its deeply caring nature is an inheritance from our long history that provides the substance for our reactions to new challenges.

For me, caring for France means combating all those things that would tear our country apart, that would cause it to retreat into its own shell, and which put us at risk of civil war. Caring for France means defending freedom of conscience, a shared culture, and our demanding but benevolent nation.

At the very time when we want to take up the gauntlet of the new world, threats that we believed belonged to a bygone age are resurfacing—both external aggressions such as terrorist attacks, and the specter of identity crises.

We must not, of course, yield to hysteria. In this regard, the dignity demonstrated by the families of successive victims of terrorist attacks has been a constant lesson to me.

We have an enemy—ISIS. We must fight that enemy relentlessly, both within our borders and beyond. However, this in no way provides justification for muddying the issues or being driven apart by tangential quarrels.

The fact that many people, young and not so young, who were born in France can tie their destiny to the murderous strategy of a totalitarian regime stems from a complex rationale. Undoubtedly, we fail to seize all aspects of that way of thinking. Gilles Kepel, Olivier Roy, and a number of others have, through their studies and fieldwork, shed light on this situation: the ideological, religious, and political agenda professed by ISIS, consisting of manipulating people's imaginations, exploiting personal frailties or even neuroses, and, lastly, capitalizing on resentment or hatred of our Republic. There are several motives, and they require responses extending beyond the essential focus on security. The situation constitutes a challenge to our civilization, posed by those in our country who have made that choice or who are tempted by extremism.

More broadly speaking, the social disintegration that we are currently seeing fuels an identity crisis, which in turn paralyzes our ability to act with a single voice.

This is because, for over thirty years now, our country has not been able to solve the problem of mass unemployment, or to prevent veritable ghettos forming in our towns. Our country is no longer able to give hope to millions of young people, whose parents have themselves often been unemployed for many years. For these reasons, we have allowed doubt, and even hatred of the Republic, to set in. It is in this context that I have spoken more than once of betrayal by our political and financial elites. Because there has been neither the willingness nor the courage to face up to these problems. We have left our compatriots to suffer the consequences of our own inadequacies.

However, for all those who make a career out of our collective concerns, we must begin by reiterating a few basic principles.

In our country, every citizen is free to have religious beliefs or not, and they must continue to have that freedom.

Every citizen is free to practice a religion or not, with a level of fervor that corresponds to their innermost feelings. The secular principle in France is a freedom rather than a restriction. Its aim is to enable everyone to be integrated into community life, and not to combat a certain religion, still less to give rise to exclusion or victimization. It is a foundation and not an impediment. How can we ask our compatriots to believe in the Republic of France if some individuals are exploiting one of our founding principles, secularism, to tell them that they have no place here?

Nevertheless, while freedom of conscience is boundless, we must be uncompromising as regards compliance with and respect for the laws of our country. There are certain things that are not negotiable in France. We do not negotiate on basic principles of civility and citizenship. We do not negotiate on gender equality. We do not negotiate our complete rejection of anti–Semitism, racism, and the stigmatization of ethnic origins.

Let us be honest. While extremism may be at work in other religions, the issue that concerns our society today involves Islam. We need to approach the subject with rigor, side by side, in a levelheaded way.

We are faced with a choice, and that choice has presented itself several times during the course of our history. Do we want to fight against a religion, to exclude it, or rather do we want to build a place for it within the French nation, giving it full support to integrate into our society? In the past, we have often made mistakes—and our nation nurses painful memories of the religious wars that ravaged its towns and countryside, and that almost led to its complete downfall.

In contrast, we have also managed to find a place for other religions in France. Judaism has developed in France against a backdrop of respect and love for the Republic. That is a fine example of what our history and political choices have been able to achieve.

We must not fall into the trap that ISIS is setting us by rushing headlong into the abyss of civil war.

The Catholic bishops of France have understood this better than many political leaders—the dignity of their reactions after the attack at Saint-Étienne-du-Rouvray is a perfect illustration of this.

There have been several proposals concerning the provisions that should be made for Islam in France: to enable Muslims to be better represented, and to be more engaged in municipal life. To guarantee that they can more easily and independently finance places of worship, and provide support for those imams who cherish the rules and values of the Republic. I believe that these proposals are going in the right direction, and I therefore intend to lend them my support.

If we truly want to make an official place for Islam in France, let us enable Muslims living in our country to assume their responsibilities with full transparency, and help them to worship with dignity. We must also help them by releasing them from ties with foreign countries, severing links with covert organizations and unacceptable sources of finance. Most importantly of all, we must not concede any ground out of convenience, as might have been the case in the past.

Let us, together, devote ourselves to the fight against radical Islamism, which aims to impose itself in certain districts, and which holds itself to be above the Republic and its laws. How can we do this? Not by tabling new laws — we already have them. Now we need to implement them, by dismantling organizations that preach hatred of the Republic, of our values, of what we are and what sustains us.

A number of Salafist associations are waging a cultural war all over France, and they are doing it through young people. They are occupying the terrain that has been deserted by the Republic. They provide help and assistance — in the absence of public services. We must not shy away from waging an uncompromising battle against them in return. We have, at the grassroots level, those who defend secularism, women's rights, and the rules of the Republic, and we do not have the right to abandon them. Our duty is to aid them — because it is these defenders who will, in close collaboration with public services, be able to restore the Republic.

The duty of the state and its representatives is to be unbending. To demand, where required, that the fundamental principles of the nation be reaffirmed before a place of worship may be opened; to ask for clarifications and elucidations regarding radical sermons. And, if necessary, to close down and to prohibit, in accordance with constitutional requirements.

Next, we need to offer a future to the neighborhoods that we have far too frequently neglected, either by allowing social and economic problems to converge there, or as a result of policies dealing only with the symptoms of adversity that haunt these areas rather than with the root causes. We have worked hard on new ways of tackling urban planning. This was an absolute necessity, and remarkable progress has been made in many localities. But we have simply worked on the places and not the people—and we have consigned those people to a kind of home detention. We told them: "We're going to regenerate your neighborhood, but you won't have access to schools in the center of town, or access to public transport; access to cultural activities will be problematic; access to on-the-job training or university is going to be extremely difficult, and as for access to employment … Don't ask too much!"

Recovering our underprivileged neighborhoods is crucial. Taking a firm hand with enemies of the Republic cannot suffice. We need to go back into these districts, and provide the inhabitants with opportunities, mobility, and dignity. And give them a true place, and a feeling of belonging to a dynamic and supportive community, which is united around the same values. This means mobility both in terms of schooling and working life, access to cultural activities, entertainment, and so on. To provide the meaning that has been usurped by certain religious experiences or extremist policies.

Our task will be difficult and will take time—it will be demanding for all of us. In my view, the task is an essential one, despite the fact that belonging to the Republic and to a religion are two separate matters. In our times, we need to place our steadfast commitment to our shared mission and respect for others above beliefs, whatever they might be.

It boils down to this: yielding to nothing as regards propaganda of division and hatred, and doing everything possible to uphold freedom. Helping Islam to sculpt its place in the Republic, but relinquishing none of our principles, and combating all forms of "communitarianism".

The above, however, is not enough. The country can only stand tall and move courageously forward if we know from whence we came. Heritage is the bedrock of our nation. Heritage enables each and every one of us to be conscious of where we come from and where we are going, in a modern age when life unfolds at breakneck speed. We are on shifting ground—sometimes for better, sometimes for worse.

We are nothing, and we cannot make anything of ourselves, until we consent to receive. Until we accept that we have to learn what others before us have learnt. We cannot fashion France, and we cannot perceive our role within the nation, until we find our place in its history, its culture, its roots, and its illustrious figures: Clovis and Henri IV, kings of France, and Napoleon, Danton, Gambetta, de Gaulle, Joan of Arc, the Army of Year II, the Senegalese Tirailleurs, the members of the Resistance—all those who have left their mark on the history of our country.

France is a fusion of its component elements. One cannot at the same time wish to be French and try to erase the past. Our history and our culture, everything that previous generations have to offer us, form our common foundation. The past is where our future begins, which is why the heroes encapsulated in the Republic are still our contemporaries: the primary school teacher, the high school teacher, the professor, the apprentice master, and equally even the CEO who passes on knowledge—all those people who choose to devote time to others and convey the essence of who we are.

Our culture is what rallies us. It unites us. It must not be elitist. On the contrary, doors must be open to all. Many times, I have observed that a reference to a poem or a literary text can stir up emotions and break down barriers. The same emotion that surfaces at public meetings when I refer to Gide or Aragon. The emotion I felt when I heard Abd al Malik cite Camus.

This inheritance is our weapon against divisiveness, against extremism, and against fatalism.

But passing on our culture, our emotions, and our sense of wonder consists of even more than this. It means that together we can rediscover the spice of life. We have lost touch with our customs—such as those that I personally came to know in the mountains, at my aunts' homes in the Pyrenees—including a local solidarity that refused to allow others to be lonely and isolated, that kept the older generation by our side. Along the way, we have lost track of our fundamental ability to care.

It is not up to politics to give meaning to our lives. And it is hard to see how politics, even if it were transformed into a doctrine of care, could purport to be a substitute for worship, or even for beliefs. But if we belong to the Republic, on the other hand, we cannot forget fraternity. It is the third word of our motto *"Liberté, égalité, fraternité"*, often considered to be the most obscure of the three, although it brings together liberty and equality in a sort of friendly benevolence that surpasses origins. The French citizens who devote their time and get involved in voluntary associations, and who donate to good causes every single year, know this very well indeed. Fraternity, which does not tolerate exclusion, forms the invisible heart of what France strives to be.

Intrinsically, something is missing for each of us individually, and for society as a whole. Changes in Western society seem to have plunged us into a form of acquiescent misery. Everyone is assigned a functional role, no matter whether in the name of the "market" or the "state".

The mysteries of life, the ability to transcend limitations, the importance of personal relationships, living our daily lives thoughtfully—things that go beyond money, social position, or efficiency—seem to have been lost forever.

Whatever their own personal quest, French people will be disaffected if they can no longer play a part in a political arena that is now beyond their control—the problem of deprived areas. But making a contribution is not only casting one's vote, running for office, drafting a manifesto, nor yet implementing it. Politics must foster our values. And those values are not limited to efficiency. They are something different. Lives are ruined in the name of business efficiency. In certain companies, with their Gordian complexity, nobody knows who is in charge or who is under orders. The people who work there—whether office workers or their managers—seem propelled by an invisible engine for which no one has the instruction manual. This kind of dehumanization, a race for "optimization" at all costs, can have dramatic consequences.

Caring for France also means caring about its values. This basic aim has formed our immigration policy for decades. Intrinsic in the welcome that France provides is not only generosity, or tradition; it is a shared desire to build a joint destiny where others are seen as enhancing our lives—a deeply felt necessity. We stretch out our hands to the newcomer who has decided to contribute to a unique common destiny and to fully embrace it.

Every year, 200,000 foreign nationals move to our country. Among them, nearly half were born in a European country, and almost a third in Africa.

Concerning asylum in particular, we must find ways to review how the large numbers of requests are handled. Application processing times must be significantly reduced, including by reorganizing the system of permits and the allocation of cross-border competencies. People who are entitled to protection from France must be welcomed, given access to training, and be granted assistance swiftly. They have a right to this. However, once the fast-track procedure has been completed, all those not eligible to remain in France in the light of the asylum criteria should be escorted to the border.

I want to say this clearly, without subterfuge: the humanitarian treatment of refugees does not mean allowing the rest of the world to believe that we will host anyone at all, indiscriminately, while granting residency permits in dribs and drabs upon the culmination of never-ending bureaucratic procedures. When we do that, we are, in fact, being incredibly inhuman—we allow applicants to enter our country for many months until processing of their applications has been completed, and then we elect to deport most of them. In the meantime, they have made a home, and sometimes have had children or got married. So the deportation orders are not executed, and the people concerned enter a limbo, without papers, and are therefore very likely to become dropouts. As a result of the lack of transparency in our aims, and an ineffective policy, the outcome is the opposite of what our traditions of welcoming others would call for. Demonstrating humanity means assuming our role, handling applications swiftly, and giving clear answers to those concerned.

Asylum-seekers cross deserts and the Mediterranean in horrendous conditions. We must put an end to this human and moral disgrace. Let's be straight about this—we are at fault here. Although the law, our own law, requires us to examine asylum applications, we do not authorize applicants to enter France legally. Naturally, they come here anyway. Thousands die on the journey, and we are partly responsible for this. Applications for asylum should be examined nearer to conflict zones, in the neighboring countries. The classic response to this solution is that the consulates are unprepared. This needs to change—it is a question of dignity and efficiency. As is the revision of the absurd Dublin system that obliges the states on the borders of the European Union to be the first to process asylum applications, and that engenders, at high cost, a distressing and vicious circle of movement because the refugees, who know that the neighboring countries will not allow them entry, always end up by coming back to central Europe—to France, Germany, and Italy.

Aside from the question of refugees, we must facilitate procedures for those who want to integrate into our society. It is unacceptable that people who wish to live on French soil or to become French citizens should spend hours in line, sent from office to office, hoping desperately that a door will open after six months or a year of being tied up in red tape. If the criteria are clearly set out, the processing of applications should take no more than two or three months. This is how I conceive of a benevolent nation.

The corollary of benevolence: expectations and requirements. France cannot host everyone regardless of the circumstances, because French values—those freedoms that I have described—are non-negotiable. Come what may. And none among our number, by cloaking themselves in magnanimity or 'otherness', may claim that gender equality, freedom of conscience, and religious freedom, including the freedom to be atheist, can be compromised. France shows its greatness when it offers these freedoms to those who come into the fold. Every person who arrives in our country must therefore undertake to observe those values—and to defend them. In return, they must benefit from social inclusion and full protection, without having their "loyalty" or "allegiance" constantly called into question by certain quarters.

I do not believe that French values are about to disappear. France is not weak. France does not need to defend what it is—stating the position will suffice. What we are missing today, and which gives us this uncomfortable and pervasive feeling of being disloyal to ourselves, are the means to inject vigor, color, and brilliance into politics. For this, we need imagination, continuing energy, and patience. We need a taste for the future. All of these virtues are tangibly present, albeit seemingly dormant or paralyzed. In truth, it would take very little to come to terms with ourselves.

CHAPTER THIRTEEN

Protecting French citizens

There are many political leaders who construct their narrative by exploiting national frailties. We hear this all the time. For my part, I am convinced that they are deceiving themselves, and that, in turn, they are deceiving the French people.

Of course, times are hard, and contemporary history has many sad stories to tell—France has been affected by the most abhorrent terrorist attacks, it is undergoing a sea change in its society, and it has been unsettled by the new directions taken at global level. But France is not a house of cards. For centuries, we have been seated at the table of the great powers of this world. We have overcome far more daunting obstacles. We have a dynamic demographic profile, a proven propensity for inclusion, an unequaled cultural heritage, and an unparalleled will.

We now owe it to ourselves to reassure the French people in the face of current threats. The state protects its citizens, and that is its primary role: to protect the freedoms of all in the face of fear.

We live in a country that is waging a determined combat against ISIS. Added to this are the daily outbreaks of violence and vilification that have been the norm for many years now, and the mounting tensions in certain city neighborhoods. There are many disparate fronts, and we have to live with continuing risks.

Among the most dangerous illusions today is the belief that we can eliminate this evil by using blockades, by withdrawing entitlements, by keeping detailed records about the whole population, by building camps, or by "spurning or disregarding human rights"—to paraphrase the words of the 1789 Declaration of Human and Civic Rights.

There is something hollow and disturbing about the many proposals that have been presented since the terrorist attacks. As in other domains, the French people are, in my view, overcoming their concerns and demonstrating a calm, a strength, and a resolution that is at odds with the disorderly panic of one section of the political class. Ideas from the traditional Right as well as the extreme Right have been amalgamated. In a hotly disputed space, candidates aspiring to succeed such figures as General de Gaulle or the polymath Poincaré find a variety of unproductive areas in which to profess their feigned interest: school-canteen menus, the length of clothing, or the ways of acquiring or withdrawing French nationality.

In so doing, and whatever the merits of such and

such a proposal—about which we ought to be able to have an open discussion—these political leaders at the same time commit a political error, a moral error, and a misinterpretation of history.

No country—and especially not ours—has ever overcome a major watershed by denying the laws that founded it, and still less the spirit of those laws. Any combat is fueled by pride and an affirmation of what one is, but also what is in no one's power to take away from us. From a strictly practical point of view, the anti-terrorist battery at our disposal is sufficient. We have no need to add extraordinary courts, internment camps, or who knows what kind of "presumption of nationality". As we know very well, the restriction of freedoms for all, or stripping citizens of their dignity, has never led to heightened security. Crimes did not increase in number after the death penalty was withdrawn, or when lawyers were allowed to assist suspects held in custody. I hold these misapprehensions to be unhelpful, and even deeply harmful. If we follow this path, the nation will be just as exposed to risk, but the face of France will have been affected in the process.

I hear some who say that they want to send all persons on whom we hold an "S" file (indicating that they are a threat to national security) to prison, so as to prevent them causing harm. Those same voices explain, as if to reassure us, that only the most "dangerous" of the persons concerned would be imprisoned. Except that no one explains how the level of danger would be assessed. And they fail to add that our intelligence services—which cannot be accused of laxity or amateur behavior—advise against taking such measures. It is not by making dangerous proposals that we reduce the threat. Proposing to systematically imprison the women and men listed in those files is to strip our intelligence of its effectiveness, but it also means moving from a state that upholds the rule of law to a police state. It is at the same time ineffective and undemocratic.

Our country stands apart from others. It will be our undoing if we take a path that is not our own in such difficult times. We must defend what is unique about France, its virtues, and its message through the ages. It is for this reason that at critical times, on fundamental matters, its message still rings out loud and clear on the world stage. That voice categorically refutes excesses that do not serve humanity.

The French identity lies there, and not elsewhere. I am struck by the paradox according to which the self-proclaimed heralds of national identity serve a cause which is not that of France, but that of their own delusions, thereby degrading our nation.

It is for this reason, too, that we must prepare, together and as soon as possible, to withdraw from the state of emergency. It was indispensable in the days following the terrorist attacks. It allowed immediate measures to be taken under conditions that would not have been permissible within another legal framework. I do not claim that it should never be implemented again if dramatic circumstances were to require its redeployment. However, its endless extension, as we all know, is very problematic.

We cannot live in a permanent state of emergency. We need to return to ordinary law, as strengthened by the legislator, and take action with the right tools. We have a whole legislative framework that will enable us to deal properly with our situation over the long term.

This does not mean that we should accommodate behavior or statements, notably in the name of religion, that go against our principles. The only way of healing the rift being caused by terrorism is to have no truck with those who would be its advocates. In order to do this, we must mobilize the whole of civil society and gain support for future plans based on trust. If that trust is betrayed, sanctions must be applied, and those sanctions must be harsh. Nothing would be worse than imprisoning whole swathes of the French population because of suspicion caused by propaganda disseminated by a minority, and because of the crimes of the few.

Here, too, we must get out of the habit of having constant recourse to the law and making incessant changes to our body of criminal law. Success will come rather from reorganizing the various sections of the police and the courts, and from reallocating resources, based on a preparatory examination of their systems by national representatives.

Each and every person has a right to be safe. How can that basic freedom, a primary responsibility of a state based on justice and integrity, be guaranteed?

The army can only be the ultimate option. It is not the natural means to discipline young people, nor is it the way to maintain order in our country. Its purpose is combat. The calls from many political leaders for an ever-increasing engagement of the army in France are a homage to these men and women who have for so long carried their heavy burden, throughout a series of reforms and restructuring schemes that few civil administrations would be capable of bringing to fruition, provoking sincere admiration from all of us. The fact remains that the army is not designed to compensate for failings in national-security measures or the shortcomings of our educational system. The army's duties can be extended temporarily. The Operational Reserve can be increased, although the contractual aspects of such an undertaking should be considered carefully, in terms of obligations, duration, and benefits. It is inconceivable and dangerous that reserves should be used to mask fundamental problems.

Hence Operation Sentinel, which led to the deployment of almost 10,000 soldiers on active service in France, was necessary to protect the country and reassure the population. It is neither realistic nor desirable to end this operation in coming months, but we must, on the one hand, preserve the current configuration of our army after Sentinel has ended, and, on the other, prepare quickly for the transition, and swell the ranks of the police force by means of a wider recruitment program.

More broadly, current security measures were put in place at a time when terrorism was not a major threat to the French people, when forms of crime were different from those we are experiencing today. It is important to understand that the fight against terrorism requires a completely different approach if we are to act effectively. It requires bonds of trust to be established with the population. A continuing police presence in our country is now a necessity. Action must involve our citizens, because proximity is the only way to collect information, and to identify and monitor dangerous individuals.

In fact, combating terrorism is first and foremost a battle for information, which requires meticulous and discreet police work: none of this would be possible if we decided to imprison the people who are the subject of our surveillance measures.

Regarding the work of our security forces, we need to recognize that we have committed errors in the past and that they have still not been remedied.

We have made mistakes. In the first place we made mistakes regarding the way in which the police force is organized. We are now suffering the consequences of having almost entirely withdrawn resources for grassroots internal intelligence services. That decision had pernicious effects, because a significant component of operational effectiveness against terrorist networks is the capacity to gather information from our towns and cities, and even from the different districts of those towns and cities. So we need to go beyond the reforms of the last few years, and restore truly effective grassroots intelligence services.

We have also failed to make the best use of information

circulating on the Internet and data collected by various government bodies. As well as addressing the coordination issues—which must be resolved—we need to create a central big-data intelligence-processing unit, as have the British or the Americans. Such a unit would report directly to the Defense Council, because it would enable high-level IT intelligence to be centralized. This is a vital complement to intelligence in the field gathered from monitoring individuals.

At the same time, we are suffering the consequences of ideological decisions taken more than ten years ago to eliminate community policing. Unlike the caricatures that have been proffered, community policing, put in place by Lionel Jospin and Jean-Pierre Chevènement, was neither the fruit of utopian laxity nor a communications subterfuge.

Whatever we decide to call it, policing on a local level to protect our compatriots must undoubtedly be put back on the agenda. Of course, the new situation needs to be taken into account: levels of violence and petty crime in certain disadvantaged areas are far higher than twenty years ago. Above all, we need to ensure that channels between police and the courts are more effective.

This new community policing must be given time— maintained in the long term—and it must be allocated human and financial resources. Local police must be allowed to establish bonds of trust with the French people. This is not a sign of weakness, but of foresight. Police officers assigned to these duties are public officials gaining a deeper knowledge of their area, who have time to gather information needed and who, when necessary, can identify dangerous individuals early on, while they are in the course of being radicalized.

Clearly, these reforms require swift reorganization and additional resources. Over and above the 9,000 staff currently being recruited, 10,000 police officers need to be taken on within the next three years.

However, this will not resolve the difficulties underscored by police officers when they took to the streets and demonstrated after the appalling attack at Viry-Châtillon.

Many police officers feel that they have to work in difficult conditions without being properly equipped, as a result of continuing budget constraints and certain teams not being included in the recruitment drives of recent years. The impression that underprivileged neighborhoods have been abandoned by the upper echelons of the police is unacceptable to the men and women in the field.

Here, too, we see the direct consequences of the lack of resources devoted to our system of justice. Courts and prisons are unable to provide an appropriate response to crime due to inadequate means — especially in the most difficult areas. This, in turn, weakens the credibility of police on the streets. Once it is obvious, as is the case in certain regions, that the Public Prosecutor will not apply for a warrant if the prison term would be under two years, the credibility of the whole criminal-justice system is called into question.

The answer is for the police force and the judiciary to focus on specific issues: at present, they are unable to combat all types of crime at all levels.

The traditional political response is to be intransigent—at all times and in all regards. This is, of course, illusory. The reality is that the police, the judiciary, and the prison service are being asked to do more and more all the time. They are among the public servants that have the most difficult working conditions to deal with. We need to increase resources for them, and to be uncompromising about our priorities: combating crime in all its forms, and eradicating no-go areas.

At the same time, however, we should begin a mature and transparent inquiry into sentencing goals. What are we expecting from criminal punishment? Taking those who have broken the law out of the community for a given length of time is not always the most effective measure for our society. Theft, for example, without aggravating circumstances, is currently punished by a three-year prison term. Could we not rather envisage reparation measures for victims, and a fine if the proceeds of the crime are below a certain amount? Similarly, should the possession and use of cannabis below a certain quantity, or less serious road offences (failure to hold car insurance, for example), necessarily fall under the jurisdiction of the criminal courts? We might feel that the range of punishments applied for minor offences would be adequate.

With regard to these issues, I refuse to allow myself to be accused of laxity. Let no one make any mistake about this: I have no sympathy for reckless drivers or drug abuse. My view is simply that we ought to listen to police officers, lawyers, and the judiciary—who are the first to explain how pointless it is to systematically punish the use of cannabis while a heavy fine, payable immediately, would save a great deal of time for the police and the courts, and be far more dissuasive than a hypothetical prison sentence that everyone knows will not be enforced.

On the other hand, I think it is essential that punishments, of whatever sort, be applied immediately and as first intended. Today, a judge giving an offender a two-year prison sentence knows that the sentence will first be examined by another judge, who will consider alternatives to prison. What is the sense of that? It is as difficult to understand for victims, and for our citizens, as it is for offenders. Prison sentences must be served. Sentencing must be taken seriously again—it is the word of the law, and must be an expression of its authority. At the same time, should we not also give the idea of prevention a chance? It has been left by the wayside. We need to step up the presence of adults (such as educators and volunteers) to support young people in disadvantaged neighborhoods, and prevent them crossing the line and being sucked into the "crime-prison-repeat offender" spiral.

The requisite state control over justice and security requires sufficient resources to be committed.

We have to win back the ground and hold on to it.

The commitment must also be a long-term one. In the last ten years, our investment has waxed and waned, dictated by events. Now we must get fully behind these priorities and, by means of a five-year framework law, set out the undertakings that the nation needs to fulfill.

Lastly, in order to be fully effective, we need to ensure that the whole of society shoulders its responsibilities. Everyone must have a place in strengthening the country's security. Obviously, this does not mean fomenting a climate of suspicion, but absorbing the idea that the state is not the only stakeholder in security matters. Everyone has a role to play in identifying threats: associations working with young people, teachers who take children on school trips, business leaders who organize seminars. We must be more vigilant about any unusual activity or suspicious behavior. It is now vital to have first-aid training, to know how to react in the event of an attack and how to contact the police without delay.

In the current situation, operational reserves play a fundamental albeit non-exclusive role. This does not mean that we should reintroduce mandatory military service for all. It would not be beneficial for our young people, and runs contrary to having a professional army. On the other hand, volunteer training for between 30,000 and 50,000 young men and women in reserve corps would enable them to make their own contribution to this essential transformation.

CHAPTER FOURTEEN

Taking control of our destiny

We are deeply immersed in the world—whether we like it or not. Millions of French people live and travel abroad. We have French territories on almost every continent. Our language is spoken in every corner of the planet.

And the world also comes to us: tens of millions of tourists visit our country each year. Two million French citizens are employed by the 20,000 foreign companies located in France. What is more, the work of millions of our compatriots is directly linked with globalization—Airbus in Toulouse, helicopter production in Marseille, turbines in Belfort, and undersea cables in Calais. These firms all serve foreign clients. We depend on globalization.

Our key challenges today are global: terrorism, migration, and so the list goes on. Obviously, we share the same planet, which ought to mean that we work together to preserve biodiversity and address climate change. The transformations under way will have direct consequences for us and our children. If we fail to take collective action, the ensuing disease and conflict will gradually destroy our planet: our most precious shared asset.

So it is clear that we cannot remain oblivious to the world—for we are part and parcel of it. Our international efforts are a prerequisite for taking control of our destiny, now that we are so inextricably linked with others.

Actually, France has never thought of itself without thinking of others. Sometimes, this leads them to view us with irritation. On the other hand, it also explains why, when France expresses no opinion on a certain subject, our neighbors and partners ask: "But what is France doing? What does France say?" The French dream has always been at the same time a universal dream. Our thinking has always been on a global scale. France is one of the few countries to take action when Christians in the Middle East are threatened, or to protest for the survival of Benghazi, or to become indignant over the martyrs of Aleppo or at crimes committed in Timbuktu.

Over time, this cultivated the belief that our country had a vocation to shine a light on the way of the world, to be the bearers of a universal humanist message, inviting all others to follow our example and to form links with our people, our model, and our values. Today's globalization suits us less well. It sometimes fails to correspond to our values—which in turn leads us to be distrustful, and tempts us to close our doors. We may be troubled by a temptation to withdraw and to desert others. I understand these fears and misapprehensions. I hear anger, too, about the way the world is going. But I believe that France cannot continue to be France if it leaves its role in the world by the wayside.

First and foremost, we have a history. We are a former colonial power with roots in every continent. We have a language spoken by 275 million people, and a special relationship with the African continent and the Middle East.

We are an international, maritime, diplomatic, and military power. We are one of the five permanent members of the United Nations Security Council—and will be the only member from the European Union once Brexit has been completed. We have nuclear weapons, and are capable of dispatching armed forces all over the world. This inevitably leads us to play a role. However, it also means that we need to demonstrate the highest levels of responsibility. It is for this reason that I recommend that our intervention should be situated within the scope of United Nations mandates. It is both more effective and more in line with our historic view of multilateralism. It guarantees us a balance that no temporary alliance could provide.

Because we have a duty to serve as an example. If France had such influence in the past, it was because it was respected as an independent, non-aggressive country, a country which at that time benefited from a great deal of tangible popularity all over the world. This was the case, for example, when we refused to go to war in Iraq with George W. Bush and Tony Blair. Today, however, France's image is somewhat tarnished. Many of our controversies are misunderstood and have changed the way people see us. Our presence in Mali is regarded with mistrust by much of the African youth, while interventions in Libya and the Sahel have been opposed.

I would like us to come together and agree that a degree of realism is now needed. We cannot devise international strategies independently of what we are doing at home. I am struck by the fact that our international public voice has remained the same, despite the fact that our situation has changed. We are asking others to believe that we have the means to carry out financial and military interventions all over the world. Are we being realistic? Can we continue to make proposals, to pontificate, and even reprimand, as if our finances were in order, as if our interventions were always crowned with success, as if our leaders were popular and our reputation intact? It leaves us open to dangers, misconceptions, and errors that sometimes occupy the realms of the ridiculous. In order to take effective action, we first of all need to be coherent.

At the other extreme, too many have brushed aside the very idea of France having its own unique and relevant position. Because they regard France as being old-fashioned, unable to recover, or condemned to fade away in the midst of the European Union or NATO. Those voices are wrong, too. We must continue to brandish our special conception of freedom, humanity, justice, and honor all over the globe. But we cannot do this without being realistic—without at the same time making the efforts to be rigorous, efficient, and moral that we keep asking the rest of the world to make.

This is also why our action, without being diminished, should in my view be far more integrated into the European framework, in particular through an indispensable strategic dialogue with Germany.

We must also set more exacting standards for ourselves—and that includes being less partisan. For too long, we have appeared to focus on our own interests, such as the sale of weapons or the profits of tour operators, rather than on the needs of those countries we purport to support. Or to assuage our consciences by ignoring those needs completely.

We have supported dictatorships and inept regimes—and we continue to do so—despite the fact that they are utterly contrary to our values.

France must retain the special and independent position that enables it to enter into constructive dialogue with others. The very nature of diplomacy is to be able to have discussions with those with whom we might disagree. However, that dialogue must not cause us to sacrifice our values, take the easy way out, or be complacent. Although realism is indispensable, principles are just as important, and a degree of modesty would do us no harm.

We would also benefit from examining, in as objective a way as possible, French military operations in the last twenty years. Parliament only does this when forced to do so by scandal or rising emotions. Despite this, I am convinced that there is a place for carrying out a thorough assessment and a rational review of both overarching policies and of processes.

———

Coming back to the present, and taking control of our destiny, I see the key issue as our external security and the need to combat our enemy, ISIS, by directing all means at our disposal against the risks it represents. Terrorism and radical political Islamism are flourishing on our borders to the east and to the south. Our diplomatic and military action must therefore be focused on maintaining security in North Africa and the Mediterranean in the face of regional crises.

The current priority is to make headway against the Islamic state on the ground, in Mosul and Raqqa, amongst other places. To prevent any massacre of civilians, as we saw in Aleppo. To stabilize the region, and in particular Lebanon, a country so close to French hearts and so often marked by war and exile. Our presence is completely necessary and fully justified. However, here too our action should form part of a clear mandate from the United Nations.

Nevertheless, in these countries, military conflict can only be resolved if we can reach a political solution, even if it is a temporary one. I have strong reservations about whether armed conflict is appropriate when launched with no political options in place in the country concerned—we have paid a high price for this in the last fifteen years in situations such as Iraq or Libya. France and its European partners must be vigilant in this respect when dealing with all current and future crises.

In Syria, France shouldered its responsibilities in

diplomatic and military terms, but has been gradually isolated, for various reasons, in particular by the Russians and the Americans, while Turkey, Iran, and a number of Gulf states each defended their own interests. It is by reaching a fair balance among all parties that peace can be re-established there. Here, the German position could be an example to us, and we will gain much if we act in clear concert with that country.

Regarding Libya, I have serious concerns. The country has supplied all those who, in the Sahel, pledged allegiance to ISIS or Al-Qaeda. Weakened on other fronts, ISIS is now attempting to make Libya its home base. It is from this country, too, that most refugees and migrants leave for Europe. It would be very grave indeed if Libya were to be taken by the terrorists: first of all, for the local populations; next, because it would increase migrant pressure on the European continent. It would offer ISIS financial reserves, in particular those generated from crude-oil production, on the eastern borders of Libya. Lastly, it would threaten neighboring countries, in particular Tunisia—a fragile democracy that has played a significant trailblazing role since the Arab Spring. It is for this reason that I was determined to make my first international visit as leader of *En Marche!* to Tunisia. European diplomatic action, hand in hand with regional allies, is needed in Libya. We must also understand the importance of working with Algeria and Egypt, who in this case have the same interests as ourselves, both in the short and medium terms.

For these reasons, North African and Mediterranean

politics need to be repositioned to form the very hub of our diplomacy. We must reclaim our historical role and our freedom of action, and we must be able to maintain exacting but continuing relationships with all actors in this region. With Saudi Arabia and Qatar, the relationship should be political as well as economic, and all subjects—including support by these countries or their citizens for organizations that destabilize the region—must be broached.

At the same time, Iran should be supported in its more open business agenda and its return to the international arena—provided, of course, that it respects, to the letter, the 2015 agreement on its nuclear program. Because in the future, if Iran were to equip itself with nuclear weapons, the entire non-proliferation policy would be called into question. The other countries in the region—Turkey, Egypt, Saudi Arabia, and so on—would then wish to follow the same route. It is therefore essential to help Iran understand that it can be a great power in the future without taking a military path. It could succeed by first imposing itself as an economic power, with a great capacity to wield influence and an important peacekeeping role.

As for Israel, it remains a diplomatic and economic ally. It is a democracy, and we must ensure that it is protected. However, at the same time, we know that lasting peace involves the recognition of a Palestinian state. Colonization policies are an error, and we must return to the spirit of the Oslo Accords. France raised concerns by voting first in favor of and then abstaining from a UNESCO resolution that emphasized Muslim connections with these holy sites and that denied Jerusalem's historic links with Judaism. In fact, France should have defended respect for all religions, and called for peaceful coexistence among them. What is happening in Jerusalem today is, in fact, the very opposite of this. We must therefore extricate ourselves from the historical debate about holy sites, rather than being hemmed in by the entrenched positions that many would like us to take.

With respect to these powers and in particular Turkey, France would gain much from taking a more strongly European approach. In the case of Turkey, it is clear that the attraction of the European model is the only counterbalance that can prevent the Turkish regime from moving towards authoritarianism and calling into question political freedoms. Turkey must not stray from Europe on security, geographical, or economic issues, taking into account its capacity to stabilize the area. But we must not be naive, because Erdogan's regime does not allow us that luxury.

North Africa, of course, stands apart in view of our history with Morocco, Algeria, and Tunisia. Millions of our compatriots come from these countries, and have strong links with them. We must not forget this. We must fully acknowledge our shared past, and build a future together. We face the same challenges, whether they relate to security, economics, or to the environment. Many of these issues need to be discussed as part of a Europe-Mediterranean dialogue.

It would no doubt be unrealistic to think that we could forge a joint Mediterranean policy, but it would be a mistake not to see that we are bound by a common destiny.

All of these countries are subject to the many risks of being destabilized, and we would suffer the first and very direct consequences if they were.

Similarly in Africa, France must continue to play the role that it has taken on in recent years in that continent, whether in Ivory Coast, the Central African Republic, or Mali. I see our military intervention in Ivory Coast under the United Nations mandate as a good example, and I deplore the fact that we left the Central African Republic, as the situation is not yet stabilized there. It is highly likely that we will be obliged to go back there in the next few years. The army's intervention in Mali was immensely useful, because it enabled that country to be saved from jihadism. On that subject, I would like to pay homage to our soldiers who are fighting in very difficult conditions.

Plainly, our role in Africa, in close cooperation with African armies and regional organizations, is to stabilize fragile zones. It is for this reason that the European Union has played a valuable role in coordinating military-training operations. However, in this corner of the globe we must also offer our support to countries who choose to take the route of openness and democracy. Because, as we know, Africa has great potential for economic success, and mutual cooperation should be stepped up in that regard.

Taking into account current French commitments—rather overstretched—and potential risks, it is clear that France must maintain influential diplomacy, an active network on the ground, and a modern and high-performing military apparatus. The army's numbers should not be reduced in the next few years, even after disengagement from Operation Sentinel has been decided upon. We must go further, and at the same time keep clearly in mind dissuasive tactics, which must be maintained whatever the cost, because they constitute our ultimate protection.

Our international security depends very much on American and Russian strategic choices. We have seen that Russia is playing an increasing role in the Middle East, and, since the Second World War, the United States has made this region the main theater of its intervention, which has benefited us more than once.

What relationship do we want to have with the Russians, our fellow Europeans? Do we want to go back to a seventy-year regime of out-and-out conflict, as we had during the Cold War? Do we really want to pursue the rather confused and conflicted relationship, currently characterized by a form of confrontation, with this major power?

We need to go back to the drawing board in our relationship with Russia. We cannot under any circumstances follow the Americans blindly (whatever happens following the election of Donald Trump), as the European Union has been more or less compelled to do for several months now. Nor can we connive with a reprehensible regime, a position preferred by some individuals on the French Right.

For my part, I will work towards an intense and frank

dialogue between us. We will not solve the problem of the Crimea in the short term. But we must work with the Russians to stabilize their relationship with Ukraine, and enable sanctions to be lifted gradually on both sides. We must find a way of reaching agreement in the Middle East in order to restore security in the region. Europe must be extremely vigilant to avoid any opportunism on the part of Russia that might see Donald Trump's election as a sign of the United States' waning interest in Europe.

We share a continent, as well as a history and even literature, with the Russians. Turgenev lived in France, Pushkin loved our country, and Chekhov and Tolstoy wielded great influence here. Twice, we faced the most terrible conflicts in world history together. At the same time, however, the Russian vision does not correspond completely to our own. It is up to us to take account of this. But we would be mistaken to cut ourselves off from this Eastern European power rather than forging a long-term relationship. In the fight against terrorism and in the energy domain, we have the makings of a productive partnership.

The question of our relationship with the United States is, in this context, more than ever a fundamental one. We are bound together by our defense of human rights and the same interests in world stability. Much was at stake during the elections in November 2016 that saw Donald Trump become president. No one can predict the consequences of that election, but it has to be admitted that the Obama years were marked by a muted tension with Europe, which escalated during the Syrian crisis.

Under President Obama, Asia was a stronger priority than Europe for the United States. This was a major repositioning in comparison to previous policies, and we are only just beginning to realize the potential consequences for us if that strategy were to be pursued by the new American administration.

Similarly, the United States is withdrawing from the Middle East and crisis zones, despite the fact that these regions had been one of their key commitments for half a century. The Obama stance in the Middle East was simple: hand responsibility over to local and regional stakeholders, and no longer take the initiative or a key role in the peace process. Following the withdrawal decided upon in Afghanistan and Iraq, as long as there is no direct threat to the United States, the Americans no longer intervene.

Close cooperation is, of course, continuing, and must be maintained. In many operational zones, American intelligence and military support are made available to France. For example, the United States does understand that the Sahel is dangerous and that our cooperation in matters of intelligence in this region is essential.

In any case, there is a need for clarification on both sides of the Atlantic, a re-assessment by the United States and by Europe, as well as a fresh approach and reinvestment. Surveillance has been an unacceptable feature of the relationship. Although it was easy for the authorities concerned to hold that the information was nothing out of the ordinary, it seems to me especially shocking when we consider that the parties in question were heads of state.

So, in the relationship between France and more broadly the European Union, on the one hand, and the United States, on the other, we find ourselves at a crossroads for the future of the planet. Is the Atlantic axis, which structures the West, and has shaped human-rights policy and peace processes since the end of the Second World War, crucial? I deeply believe that it is. However, we need to recalibrate our relationship, in view of the fact that it is so important in determining our capacity to protect our compatriots. At the time of writing, American political life has taken a new direction with the election of Donald Trump as president of the United States. Nobody knows what his first decisions will be. I know at the very least that, like his predecessors, those decisions will be constrained by realities. It is up to us to ensure that our ideas prevail. It is also up to us to take full measure of this global change.

As a result, now more than ever, we must build a ten-year European diplomatic and military strategy. Western Europe will need to stand alone more and more often in order to defend itself. We must, therefore, as one of the leading military powers in Europe, work with our European partners—not only Germany, but also the United Kingdom, which, in this field, and taking into account our links, still remains a strategic partner. Faced with risks from neighboring countries in the region, and in view of the new positions and uncertainties concerning Russia and the United States, we need to organize our collective security in a more independent manner.

———

In order to take control of our destiny, our second area of action must be all of our trade, economic, and cultural initiatives in the rest of the world. This is crucial to enabling France and Europe to have real influence, and to avoid the setbacks that can sometimes affect our country, so that our artists, our schools, our companies, and our ideas can shine all around the world.

We possess great strengths in this regard, and we have an exceptional diplomatic network to rely on. Here, I must express a conviction that goes against the choices that have been made for many years now. It is at all times more important to maintain our stock markets, our cultural centers, and our schools than to maintain diplomatic jobs. Of course, maintaining a diplomatic network is indispensable, but here, too, we could develop a more European approach, while our cultural influence would be our own domain. And it is culture that makes the French presence in a country stand out.

When I visited Tunisia, I was struck by discussions I had with political and cultural leaders. Their models were all French. They had a perfect command of the French language. Their cherished memories were stolen moments with French artists, writers, and filmmakers.

Nevertheless, I am fully aware of the damage caused over the last fifteen years by the withdrawal from policies that foster the Francophone culture, and by the lack of interest in promoting artists abroad. France betters itself and the world when its culture shines. When it supports and promotes its language and linguistic diversity. When it grants scholarships to students from every continent. When it allows people thousands of kilometers away, in the middle of another continent, to have a taste of France—in a spirit of exchange, curiosity, and mutual dialogue. Because the bonds built in this way, between the French people and our partners worldwide, are so many ramparts against ignorance and even barbarism, so many ties between these faraway citizens and ourselves.

And here I see Africa as a continent full of promise, where we must reassert and redeploy our ambitions.

Our presence cannot be limited to military and political action. We must now go further, and enable entrepreneurs and the middle classes to prosper throughout Africa. This will be the best way to stabilize African democracies in the long term. In this regard, the work carried out in 2013 by Hubert Védrine, Lionel Zinsou, Hakim El Karoui, Jean-Michel Severino, and Tidjane Thiam is still very relevant. It forms the nucleus of the strategic action that I want to be able to put in place on this continent. Traditionally, our economic presence in Africa has been built up in close collaboration with governments, in sectors such as commodities and infrastructure. It has developed with a lack of transparency that has prevented corruption from being addressed effectively on either side, and has prevented the majority of Africans from benefiting from the positive effects of the relationship.

Today, a new business elite is emerging, which is acting

as a driver for the middle classes and indeed the whole population in these African countries. By building trust with this new generation, we must strengthen our relations with Africa in a balanced way in the coming decade, without any trace of condescending behavior.

I am not going to give an exhaustive list here of every country with whom we have historical links, unique bonds, cultural exchanges, or special trade or industrial relationships. They range from Brazil to Argentina, through Colombia and Chile, from Japan to South Korea, not forgetting China and India. In the midst of transformation, India is strengthening its many ties with France, as it is with Australia—with whom we ourselves have just signed important agreements.

China, of course, occupies a special place on that list. It is a great power that is about to become the world's leading economy. Many of our compatriots know very little about China. They still see it as the world's factory, as a place for low-cost manufacturing. They see it as being responsible for the relocation of factories and the deindustrialization of France. But China is much more than that, which is why we need to change our perspective. Far from being considered a peril, China can represent an opportunity, if we provide ourselves with the means to seize it.

France has the capability, with its companies, to address the considerable challenges that China is facing (urban development, energy needs, combating pollution).

Long-standing partnerships already exist, such as in the nuclear domain.

We can make use of the special ties that bind us: the Chinese leadership has never forgotten that France was the first Western country to recognize the People's Republic of China.

However, to succeed in this ever-evolving globalization, we need Europe. In the last thirty years, the world has changed profoundly. France has, in some ways, diminished in size. New economic powers and business powers have emerged. The best way of defending our preferences and our values is therefore to have an effective European policy. And, in particular, a common trade policy. Only Europe can negotiate with China or the United States credibly and effectively. On this subject, I do not think that in future years the negotiations underway with the United States concerning a free-trade treaty will progress. On the other hand, we would benefit from deploying a proactive trade strategy and initiating discussions with the Asia-Pacific region so that we avoid leaving the Americans to act as the arbiter. The European Union is also a regulatory space where we need to place a focus on digital matters, and ensure that our preferences are taken into account, whether they concern the use of commercial or financial data, or the protection of privacy.

The third strand of action concerns our civilization. We have to rethink humanism for our times. I am convinced that the globalized world is synonymous with opportunities for many people. However, at the same time, globalization has been debased by the excesses of financial capitalism that our nation-states can no longer regulate. The Bretton Woods compromise, which, after the Second World War, enabled financial regulations to be put in place in order to create a sorely needed new financial and monetary balance, won the day. The G20, an international group bringing together the twenty largest world economies, resuscitated after the 2008 financial crisis, has not really reined in these aberrations.

Today, on the other hand, our global form of capitalism produces more inequalities than have ever been created in our developed countries. Since the 1980s, it has been the middle classes in Western economies who have been sacrificed the most in this historic change. Initially, the new elite and the middle classes in emerging economies benefited from the growth of their economies; but during the last twenty-five years, the richest 1 per cent of the population have accumulated more and more wealth.

International capitalism no longer regulates itself. Worse still, the institutions created to address the problem have not been of any benefit. And so, whether in the case of financial crises, or those sacrificed by globalization, the victims of climate change or the destruction of biodiversity, France must fight to enable us to anticipate, to prevent issues from arising, to contribute to changing international rules, and render this contemporary capitalism more human.

I do not know whether we will succeed. I do not know

whether this form of capitalism is on the verge of being condemned by the very reason of its excesses. However, I am convinced that France must take its rightful place in this essential undertaking—ensuring that human values prevail in globalization. France has every reason to succeed: its history, its principles, its strengths ... Beyond the environmental combat, France must fight to step up international regulation, apply rules to gray financing, continue to regulate financial executives' remuneration worldwide, and fly the flag of social and environmental responsibility. This undertaking must be global if we want it to be effective. It would be illusory to imagine that we could wage this war alone. The G20 is the right framework to do this, but France must, along with the European Union, promote a clear and proactive agenda in this area.

I am also convinced that we need to combat tax evasion and tax fraud at a European and global level. The OECD (Organization for Economic Co-operation and Development) and the European Union have made great strides in recent years in imposing more transparency. Nevertheless, developments in the digital economy facilitate and even encourage securities transfers and, consequently, questionable practices. Here, too, we need to take strong and clear measures. First of all, by including all countries in the Eurozone in tax convergence in the field of corporate tax. It will take ten to fifteen years, but such convergence is indispensable.

Next, we need to demand that all existing tax agreements between European Union countries and tax havens be renegotiated. Lastly, we need to ensure that all trade agreements are accompanied by tax-cooperation agreements to combat tax evasion and optimization as the method used to achieve it. Opening up trade is only sustainable, politically speaking, as long as the taxable wealth that is necessary for any redistribution does not evaporate with the movement of capital. The great Western powers will have new leaders by the close of 2017. We need to ensure that by 2020 we can lay down the foundations of new rules for globalization. This is not a battle to "prevent", or simply to "preserve", but a battle against devastating excesses, and for our common future.

In fact, the times we are currently experiencing no doubt constitute a change in the world order. Some people are tempted to see in this the end of the Western heyday; others prefer to view it as a different balance of power. Our sustained response must be to make globalization more civilized, and to base our action in the heart of a Europe that has become even more indispensable.

CHAPTER FIFTEEN

A new Europe

In order to take back control of our destiny, we need Europe. For many years, our political leaders have led us to believe that Europe is the problem, and that it is responsible for all our ills.

Do we need to remind them that we *are* Europe? We are the people that history and geography placed at the center of Europe. We created it, and we chose it. We appoint its representatives. Let us be clear about this: electing the president of the Republic of France means electing the person who is going to sit at the table of the European Council on France's behalf.

And when I survey the wider world, I am certain of two things: what brings Europeans together outweighs the issues dividing us; and we have little chance of standing up to China or the United States if we are not capable of understanding that fact.

Fundamentally, whose heirs are we?

As a political edifice, Europe is a new kid on the block. It is only sixty-five years old, and despite that fact, it is already exhausted. Over the decades, the founding fathers' ideal has become bogged down in bureaucracy. It has been misplaced among the treaties, and gone off track due to a lack of vision.

The European edifice was based on three promises: a promise of peace, a promise of prosperity, and a promise of freedom. A profoundly French venture.

The European edifice is the offspring of peace, and it consolidated that peace. For decades, it turned a dream of peace into a reality for millions of Europeans. So much so that many of us managed to believe that conflict would be no more, forgetting that conflict formed the historical undercurrent of our continent. The European dream has always been a dream of empire and unification through war: from Caesar, Charlemagne, and Napoleon, through to the Hitlerian tragedy. We must never lose sight of the fact that war is our past on this continent, and that it could also be our future if we do not build a free Europe. For the first time, we have managed to unite the continent through peace and democracy. Our European dream has taken the unprecedented form of a non-hegemonic edifice, designed to enable neighboring peoples to finally live together in peace after the terrible suffering caused by two world wars. No less important was recovery from the social trauma caused by those wars: the Holocaust, mass murder—a complete betrayal of the Western ideal.

The second original promise was that of a prosperous

Europe. Devastated by war, Europe could only conceive of a common venture on the condition that it was aimed at economic recovery. Despite the adversity of that time, Europe succeeded in building an economic and social model unequaled in other parts of the globe.

The third and last promise was that of a free Europe, with unrestricted mobility for persons and goods. Concrete examples of that mobility are the Schengen open-border zone, the academic-exchange program Erasmus, the euro single currency, and the removal of barriers such as bank charges for cross-border transactions or telephone-roaming charges.

For Europeans today, these three founding promises seem to have been betrayed.

The promise of peace has been undermined. The Syrian, Libyan, and Ukrainian crises; migrant pressure, the like of which had not been seen for sixty years; and, worst of all, the repeated terrorist attacks on our own soil have made people painfully aware that the course of history has not changed. War and conflict are not things of the past.

The promise of prosperity has been betrayed. Europe is bogged down in sluggish growth. Personally, for as long as I can remember, and ever since I became acquainted with world affairs, I have heard people talking about financial crises. At the present time, one young person out of five in the Eurozone is unemployed. In such a situation, how can we expect new generations to subscribe to the European ideal? When the euro was threatened, Europe was able to survive the emergency. However, we have to face up to the fact that austerity is not a way forward, and that reducing sovereign debt does not in any way constitute a productive political goal.

The promise of freedom has been jeopardized, too. Freedom of movement, in particular, is called into question every single day. It may be questioned for economic reasons, or on grounds of inclusion and migration flows. Or for security reasons, owing to the terrorist threat. Or, more generally, because continuing unemployment and worsening inequalities lead to citizens rejecting openness and being tempted to shut the world out and retreat into their shells.

These three promises must not be called into question. They still represent an incredibly fine venture. However, we cannot succeed in that venture if we turn our back on others.

So what has happened?

The European Union has languished and become enfeebled, and we are all to blame. There is, currently, a noticeable paucity of ideas and methods. The whole system has capitulated, and is at a standstill. Summits bringing together heads of state and of government have become a parody: getting together behind closed doors, repeating lofty principles, changing a word or two in a statement so that it sounds slightly different from the last one. The system is cut off from the world and from real life. What did the Breton farmers I have met in the last few months have to say about all this? They did not say that they were against Europe, or the common agricultural policy that is so important to us. But they explained that they were against over-regulation, against over-zealous bureaucracy, and against interventionist policies overseas, so far removed from their real needs.

The founders of Europe believed that political union would be a natural consequence of union in the economic domain, and that a European state could be created from a single market and a single currency. Half a century later, reality has dispelled that illusion. Political Europe has not happened. Any hope of it has been sorely diminished, and it is the fault of us all.

First of all, because it was our own desire to weaken Europe. Heads of state and of government have done everything they can in the last few years to put in place a weak leadership to run the European Union. They decided to create a commission with twenty-eight commissioners. This is not workable, and the organization of the commission clearly needs to be changed if we want to go back to the truly collegial nature and efficiency of the commission under Jacques Delors.

Gradually, the European Union has abandoned its vision in exchange for official procedures, confusing the aim—to unite Europe—with the technical, monetary, legal, and institutional means for union to be achieved. And so, ultimately, this part of the vision was thwarted, as were others. Seeing Europe as the source of all our problems became a reflex, whereas questioning the role of the commission or its many directives was tantamount to being a bad European.

For the French people, matters came to a head in 2005. In that year, through a referendum, we realized that Europe as it had become might no longer be the Europe for us. It had moved too far towards neoliberalism, and had become too far removed from our values. In practice, people feared losing the benefits that our country had traditionally drawn from the European Union—such as in the domain of agriculture—and were concerned about new challenges, such as immigration.

These negative feelings have been exacerbated since the 2005 referendum, in view of the fact that Europe's advocates responded to the traumatic "NO" by fleeing the arena of debate and ideas. The Greek monetary crisis revealed shortcomings of the same sort when, between the proclaimed apocalypse and the stop-gap strategy finally negotiated, the European political elite sidestepped certain discussions that were sorely needed.

Europe has become bogged down because no one takes responsibility. We French have too often believed, in our hearts, that the best way to defend our national interests was to free ourselves from the European rules that we had contributed to creating. In addition, the lack of real control over European policies has created a climate of insecurity. It is significant that, due to the lack of a suitable forum, no true political debate took place concerning the decisions that led to a situation where the single currency had permitted certain states—Greece, Italy, Spain, Portugal, and also ourselves—to live beyond their means and to court disaster. The choices made by European leaders, the practices of their administrations, the proliferation of rules, and inadequate implementation of the principle of subsidiarity ought to be subject to exacting oversight at all times. Currently, European institutions are incapable of such oversight.

They are also, broadly, unable to defend effectively the values which, beyond the economy, form the foundation of Europe. Nobody should be able to conclude that humanism stands for so little. I have always supported the Greek government's efforts to stay within Europe's monetary union. Nevertheless, I am amazed that at no time did European negotiators see fit to insist that the Greek authorities comply with the European rules that they had clearly neglected in recent years—in particular, those relating to the right of asylum. Certain recent decisions by the Hungarian government jeopardized the very principles on which Europe was founded, and were not the subject of one-tenth of the summits into which we rush headlong when taxpayers' money or the banks' financial robustness seems to be at risk. We must not consent to such compromises.

Last but not least, the European Union contributes to its own downfall when it fails to stand up for itself through an excess of conformism and a lack of vision. What can we say about the February 2016 agreement that offered the United Kingdom an 'à la carte Europe', yielding to its blackmail?

For all these reasons, I believe that we have squandered the last decade.

Brexit is the name of this crisis and the symptom of the fatigue that is pervading Europe. However, let us hope—and, as reformers, hope is our role and our duty—that it is also the beginning of an indispensable transformation.

Brexit is not a selfish act. Let us never denounce any citizen for having voted "badly": it would be nonsensical. Of course, it would be easier to "dissolve the people", as Bertolt Brecht said, than to face facts. I prefer the second alternative.

Brexit is the expression of a need for protection. It expresses a rejection of the very social model that the British political leaders have defended. Protection from a society that advocated openness, without concerning itself with the industrial, economic, and social destruction necessarily engendered by such openness when it takes place too quickly. Brexit expresses the weaknesses of a political class that found its scapegoat—Europe—and failed to explain that leaving Europe would lead to disaster. Protection from a public debate in which experts' arrogance and demagogues' lies were lumped together indiscriminately.

In this sense, Brexit is not a British crisis, but a European one. It should cause alarm bells to ring throughout the member states, and it should be a wake-up call for all those who remain blinkered to the negative effects of globalization. In fact, people fall into two almost equal camps: supporters of an open society, and those who advocate a closed society. This rift has emerged from all of the ballot boxes: the regional elections in Germany, the local elections in Italy, the Austrian presidential election, the Polish and Hungarian excesses, and, of course, here in France with the rise of the National Front.

So we have to go back to the drawing board with Europe—starting from its origins.

How can the phoenix rise again? How can a reinvigoration policy be conducted in a climate of growing skepticism?

We need to rekindle a desire for Europe—a shared undertaking for peace, reconciliation, and development. There is nothing harder to define than a collective plan, which is quickly diluted by individual interpretations. In order to succeed, we must not start out with technicalities, or complex and bureaucratic solutions. We must construct a true political plan. For many European countries, Europe is not limited to a market, but is a space with a certain idea of humanity and of entrepreneurial freedom, where progress and social justice is asserted. Those countries must re-appropriate the project for themselves, and take the necessary steps to ensure its success. That philosophy was advocated for many years by Jacques Delors. It is up to France to take the initiative and to work with Germany, Italy, and some others to set our Europe right.

We need to build this new European venture around three concepts: sovereignty, a taste for the future, and democracy.

Let us begin by accepting the diagnosis: the rift today is between those for an open society and those for a closed one. Reformists and progressivists alike must support an open society and Europe's choices.

Being an advocate for progress today is to say that our relationship with the world is not one of isolation. It means understanding that we have more to lose than to gain if we withdraw into our shells. It means convincing others that openness is only tenable if it is accompanied by protection. It means ensuring that openness can benefit all citizens, in all member states.

However, we have confused sovereignty and nationalism. I say that those who truly believe in sovereignty are pro-Europeans: Europe is our chance to recover full sovereignty. What are we talking about here? Once again, let's go back to the meaning of words to clarify matters. Sovereignty means a population freely exercising its collective choices, on its territory. And having sovereignty means being able to act effectively.

Faced with the current serious challenges, it would simply be an illusion, and a mistake, to propose to rebuild everything at the national level. Faced with an influx of migrants, the international terrorist threat, climate change, the digital transition, as well as the economic supremacy of the Americans and the Chinese, Europe is the most appropriate level at which to take action.

Who can seriously believe that we alone can control migration flows from North Africa or the Middle East? That we can regulate, alone, the North American giants with their digital platforms? That we can meet global-warming challenges alone? Or that, alone, we could negotiate balanced trade agreements with the United States or China?

In the next few years and in these different domains, we must move forward with the other twenty-six member states of the European Union. Let us stop and consider migrant flows for a moment. This subject is deeply associated with sovereignty, but action at the European level needs to be strengthened in the light of threats that are more and more global in nature. The idea put forward by some people that true protection could be provided by going back to national frontiers is completely fanciful. Do they imagine that we are going to redeploy our armies at our borders? Or close our borders with Germany, Belgium, Spain, or Italy? Is this what we really want? This path is even less relevant in view of the fact that many of the terrorists who have attacked our country in the last few months were French, and lived in France and Belgium.

In Europe, our interests converge on this point. But we need to step up action and establish a real policy—today among the twenty-eight member states, and after Brexit among the remaining twenty-seven. This presupposes investment in an effective joint border force and coastguard, and a joint identity-card system. Because whoever arrives in Lesbos or Lampedusa has a foothold in our country. Realistically, at this time, the force that we call Frontex is only able to intervene if a state requests its intervention, and it has very limited resources. Cooperation among our national forces is inadequate.

The question of borders is a fundamental one today.

However, we must deal with the question at the right level. Giving ourselves the means to protect our European borders is the appropriate response.

Making such a security policy effective also presupposes that we coordinate our actions with respect to third countries. First of all, by looking at conflict zones and migrants' countries of origin. The European Union must organize its refugee policy according to the countries of origin. Europe's error was to fail to put in place such a policy prior to the beginning of the financial crisis.

Next, we must set out a coordinated development-aid policy for those same countries, to help them manage refugee flows themselves—particularly in regions near the Syrian conflict zone. And here, too, another mistake was made when several million refugees were trapped in those countries. Europe was asked to help by the United Nations without having been proactive, and therefore without having any plans in place.

Lastly, it is clear that in the coming months we will need to broach the subject of cooperation with the United Kingdom as regards the subject of immigration. The United Kingdom's current financial contribution will not suffice: France cannot bear the burden of refugee camps alone. Even beyond financial contributions, it is imperative that the United Kingdom accepts joint responsibility, along with the European Union, for managing the problem of refugees at the union's borders.

Europe is the proper level of sovereignty protection for these matters.

Let us take another example—that of trade. A sovereign Europe will also regulate free trade and achieve a more humanized form of globalization. As minister, I initiated that fight when defending our iron and steel industry against unfair competition. I defended the need for trade policy to remain a European issue—sometimes entirely on my own, and particularly regarding the agreement with Canada—because we are stronger together. What protection could France alone put in place against China? What sort of beneficial trade agreement could such and such a country negotiate with our larger partners?

However, if we delegate responsibility for free-trade agreements to Europe, we must ensure that there is earlier and more regular participation by citizens in the European Parliament and in national parliaments. It also means heightened transparency, and, above all, more effective protection against unfair practices. I favor stepping up anti-dumping measures, which must be swifter and more powerful—as they are in the United States. We must also put in place, at a European level, foreign-investment controls in strategic sectors, to protect any industry that is essential to our sovereignty, and to guarantee European control of key technologies.

The European Union, if we are decisive about this and if we draw all the necessary conclusions, is what will enable us to build our place in the globalized world and provide us with fair protection there. This is the pillar around which we must create a new Europe.

———

The European Union also needs to be built around a taste for the future, a joint aspiration for recovery. Today, the European Union, and in particular the Eurozone, is declining due to a lack of ambition. We are crippled with doubts as a result of past crises, whereas what we need are new ambitions, and an investment policy applied at a European level.

In this regard, some voices claim that the euro has been a mistake. That would be to forget its benefits far too quickly: it protects us from currency fluctuations, stimulates trade within the Eurozone, and enables us to obtain financing under historically favorable conditions. On the other hand, it must be recognized that the failure to achieve full monetary union was an error.

Today, the euro is being weakened as a result of the widening gaps between its economies, the slow recovery, and a lack of public and private investment. Previously, in the absence of proper political direction, the euro ended up by accentuating differences between economies in the Eurozone, instead of bringing them closer together. Faced with an unprecedented crisis, the weakest economies collapsed, and the member states had to contend with the debt predicament. Today, in the absence of centralized political direction, the imbalances that have accumulated are taking time to redress, despite an unprecedented austerity policy in many European countries. In spite of the fact that the whole zone ought to be stimulated by the investments essential to its growth, harsh budgets continue to be predominant. The European Central Bank has done everything it could in the last five years, and without its determined action we would certainly find ourselves in a recession.

I will propose that Europe create a joint Eurozone fund to finance investments, to assist the regions most in difficulty, and to address crises. In fact, as levels of national debt differ across the Eurozone, there is leeway to do this with the resources available.

We need a minister of finance to oversee this for the Eurozone. That person would define priorities for the budget and would give backing to member states that carried out reforms in line with those priorities. The minister would be responsible to a Eurozone Parliament that would bring together all European parliamentarians from the Eurozone at least once a month, to ensure true democratic oversight.

At the same time, we will need to decide together to revise the rules of the game and put in place a more appropriate economic policy. The Eurozone has not returned to pre-crisis investment levels, and no economic bloc can sacrifice its future in this way. A European investment plan based on subsidies and not mainly on loans and collateral, much more powerful than the current "Juncker Plan", must be put in place as soon as possible. That plan must finance the necessary investments in fiber optics, renewable energies, energy interconnections and energy-storage technologies, education, training, and research. All future investments that can contribute to the plan will need to be dispensed from the debt and deficit objectives included in the EU Stability and Growth Pact.

Here, France has a very grave responsibility. If we want to convince our German partners to forge ahead, it is imperative that we apply reforms at home. Today's Germany has a wait-and-see attitude, and blocks many European projects due to its distrust of us. We have betrayed Germany three times. Once in 2003–2004, when we undertook to make fundamental reforms and only the Germans carried them out. Again in 2007, when we unilaterally put a stop to the agenda for public-spending reduction that France and Germany were conducting together. Then, again, by playing for time in 2013 and not taking decisive action. This is also the reason why Germany is now increasing its budgetary surplus, which is good neither for that country nor for Europe as a whole. Let us never forget that there is a place for French leadership in Europe — but that leadership means leading by example.

This being the case, it seems to me that the right way to proceed is very clear. In summer 2017, we are to present a strategy for reforms to modernize the country, and a five-year plan for reductions in current expenditure, implementing them without delay. In return, we must ask the Germans to carry out a potent budgetary-stimulus program. They must move ahead with us on the idea of a Eurozone budget, and on authorization across all Eurozone countries for investments in our future.

If we want to build an economic power reconciling

both solidarity and responsibility, we must apply reforms at state level, but at the same time it is crucial that certain Eurozone member states go further. They should give themselves ten years to achieve tax, social, and energy convergence—which will form the heart of the Eurozone, and without which it will fall apart.

All this presupposes that a genuine political decision will be taken within two years. The foundation of this European fulcrum will see these countries coming together and establishing a joint budget for the Eurozone and investment capacity that can be deployed rapidly. The two years ahead are decisive for Europe and the Eurozone. If these decisions are not taken, it is unlikely that Europe will last very long, in view of the fact that it is currently so beset by diverging interests and weakened by nationalism in many countries.

At the end of those two years, the French people will need answers. Because if we have failed, it will be essential to draw conclusions both for us and for our partners. This fight for Europe is one of the most crucial for the presidency. It is the condition of our sovereignty. And in order to succeed we must convince our European partners right now. This is what I shall do, in close collaboration with Germany and Italy in particular.

The European Union, on the other hand, remains entirely relevant. With its twenty-seven members, it will be a wider circle, but will remain a political and economic space, that of the single market and of overarching regulations. It will be the arena in which competition policy, trade policy with regard to the other great powers, the digital agenda, and energy policy will be conducted, which may require specific regulation.

If we want to make progress on matters of defense and security, we must move much faster with respect to the Schengen area, and be more ambitious in deploying border forces and coastguards, the creation of which has recently been decided upon. Together we need to establish our joint border policy, and to have an ambitious cooperation policy on intelligence and asylum.

The European Union must therefore continue to progress in its capacity to regulate and protect. Because it has the critical mass to do so. And this is in no way incompatible with the convergence needed within the Eurozone.

However, all of this will only happen if we place democracy in the pole position. We must not allow our citizens or our ideas to be monopolized by rabble-rousers or extremists. We must not make Europe into a sort of crisis-management center for a condominium that keeps trying to extend its bylaws because the neighbors don't trust each other anymore. We must not be waylaid by dogma that would prevent us from meeting the legitimate hopes and aspirations of our compatriots.

We need to take the time for discussion, and re-establish trust. It is a wide-ranging discussion, which I propose to initiate in 2017, at a key political time — that of the French, German, and Dutch elections.

I will propose the launch of democratic consultations throughout the European Union, as soon as the German elections are over, in autumn 2017. In each member state, for a period of between six and ten months, this would involve a debate on the details of the Union's action, on the policies that it implements, and the priorities that it should have. Governments and regional authorities would make their own organizational choices regarding procedures for the consultations.

The results of these consultations would enable European governments to prepare a concise roadmap, with a small number of shared challenges and specific actions, tracing out priorities for the union's action and an implementation schedule for the next five or ten years. Each state would then validate this "Plan for Europe" according to their own democratic traditions. For countries organizing a referendum, a coordinated campaign must be organized, to generate democratic debate at European level.

In this way, Europe could once again achieve legitimacy, with democratic debate reinvigorated, and involved citizens. Thus, when one member state votes against a new project, it will not be able to block the others from going ahead, because we will have decided, from the outset, that our procedures are to be changed—as Mario Monti and Sylvie Goulard proposed as a means of ensuring success. The dissenting state will simply not join in with that project. Of course, Europe will be more differentiated—it is already. But it will be differentiated in a forward-thinking way rather than by successive backtracking.

This transformation will not happen overnight. It will take years. We need to think in the long term again, and have a vision for the future. But when things take a long time to do, it is even more urgent to start doing them.

CHAPTER SIXTEEN

Returning power to those who get things done

France has placed great importance for a very long time on politics making a real difference, and on citizens being closely involved in the democratic process. Nevertheless, a democratic fatigue has taken hold. We no longer accept the so-called "system" or the ineffectiveness of public action. Nor do we agree to our destiny being taken hostage by the few.

This is not specific to France, however. Many democracies, particularly Western democracies, share the same plight. Fear of losing one's position, dread of a fragmenting world, and a fascination for extremism or provocateurs all feed into our disenchantment.

Given the above, people might put two arguments to me: "You are part of the system, so how can you read us chapter and verse about it?", or "Why would you succeed in taking action and transforming the country where so many others have failed?"

I have two answers, and they are just as direct. First, I am a product of the French meritocracy—I achieved success there, but I never went along with the traditional political system. Second, I believe that I can succeed in making changes because I am not going to try to do everything all at once—I want to set out a clear plan, and convince you of its worth. Anything I do, I will do with you by my side.

What makes our compatriots angry and leads them to reject politics is the certitude that power is in the hands of leaders they can no longer identify with, who no longer understand them, and who no longer care about them. And that is the source of all our problems.

As a result, many politicians persuade themselves that we need new rules, new laws, and some even think we need a new Constitution. Despite what they say, our country was able to flourish, a long time ago, with that same Constitution, without any storms of anger brewing.

The crucial factor is the stuff that people are made of. When the political and institutional leaders of our country went underground during the Second World War, or spent several months commanding tank regiment units, they did not behave in the way that leaders do now. It is clear that public morale, a sense of history, and leaders' human qualities are not what they used to be, and our compatriots are fully aware of it.

At his press conference on 31 January 1964, General de Gaulle said, in words that have remained famous, that a Constitution is "made of a spirit, institutions, and practice". The spirit of the institutions of the Fifth Republic, he went on to say, was born out of a necessity to "ensure that government is effective, stable, and responsible". These are the objectives that I want to embrace, and which are now accepted as historical assets for our country.

It is my conviction that French people are fed up with the promises regularly made to them that their institutions are going to be changed—either to be "remodeled", or to be "adapted to the needs of the times", or even that a "Sixth Republic" will be built. I do not believe that such changes are a priority for the French people. Such changes will not provide concrete answers to their problems. I will not deny that in certain matters—for example, the duration of the presidential mandate, the reduction in the number of members of parliament, or reforms of certain assemblies—changes to our institutions might be worthwhile. However, as a general rule, I believe that we should exercise considerable caution if we wish to radically reform our institutions or the Constitution. We will do this when the time comes.

In my opinion, it is in practice that the majority of changes need to happen. Amending the conditions for proportional representation, improving on voting procedures where appropriate, taking measures to effectively combat over-regulation and constant changes to rules—these are the kind of initiatives that will enable politics to stop navel-gazing and start serving France and the French people a little more and a little better.

The challenge is to know how our country can equip itself with public leaders who can represent it more effectively and who are able to rise to the challenges of our times. French citizens rightly feel they can no longer identify with their representatives. Only a quarter of members of parliament are women, despite the law on gender balance. Thirty-three of them are lawyers, and fifty-four are civil-service officials. Their influence in the National Assembly is disproportionate to their influence in society. On the other hand, only one member of parliament has worked as an artisan, whereas there are over three million artisans in France. Less than a dozen members of parliament come from ethnic minorities.

It is not a case of counting members of parliament according to the color of their skin or the origin of their name. But we cannot fail to be shocked by the increasing difference between the face of France and the face of its representatives. Extending proportional representation, without damaging the effectiveness of our democratic system, is obviously one solution. Of course, I am aware of the consequences of such a change: more National Front representatives would no doubt be able to become members of parliament. But how can we justify the fact that almost 30 per cent of the electorate say that they vote for the National Front, and yet it has so few representatives? What we need to do is to combat the party's ideas, rather than prevent it from being represented.

Nevertheless, we will take care not to go from one extreme to another. First of all, I deeply believe that French people are less concerned with representation than action. They want politicians to be efficient, and that's all there is to it. It is up to us to convince them that the revitalization of the world of politics will make that happen. This is why we must ensure that any reforms of voting procedures do not weaken our effectiveness, that they truly foster renewal rather than supporting actors whose allegiance is solely to parties and to the existing system.

Another way to breathe new life into politics is to regulate the holding of political appointments. We know that, from 2017, the current law will make it impossible to be a member of parliament or a senator and at the same time hold office at local level. The change is a positive one, although, as I see it, prohibiting politicians from receiving more than one salary would have been sufficient, and the question of ensuring that the territories are represented in the Senate needs to be addressed. However, this is not sufficient to foster renewal. For this reason, I believe that members of parliament should be prohibited from holding office for an extended period of time. The aim is not to sanction elected members who have experience—because politics, like everything else, requires know-how and skills. Nevertheless, when politics is no longer a vocation but a profession, political leaders no longer have commitment, and have vested interests.

In order for politics to serve the French people once again, I believe more strongly in commitment than in sanctions.

The challenge consists less of preventing elected representatives from remaining in place than of encouraging new people to enter politics—especially those who are not civil servants, politicians' colleagues, party employees, or members of the professions. And this is why we must, as a priority, address what happens before people are elected, and work directly with employees' and employers' representatives to support those who take risks, those who go out campaigning, those who want to make a commitment to our country.

Several companies, such as Michelin, have put in place measures to enable their employees to stand for election. If elected, they will be able to return to their previous posts at the end of their term in office, without losing out on any promotion opportunities or grade benefits that would have accrued had they stayed at the company.

Elected representatives who leave office must be given support: if so many of them want to remain ensconced, it is because very often they have no idea what to do next. Initiatives should be pursued to help them change careers. Our society owes them this, because these people have struggled hard on its behalf.

At the same time, we need to reinvigorate our fossilized political apparatus. This is the blind side of democratic debate. In our times, the parties have given up on fighting for the common good. They focus on their own interests—to survive, come what may. Such transgressions are not limited to the Left or the Right. It is not a question of being a demagogue or a democrat:

the people responsible come equally from the extremes and from the centrally positioned parties. The political decline facilitates the co-opting of others and back-room deals—it transforms people who were dedicated to a cause into members of an old guard.

If the parties fail to turn the tide and to remodel themselves, representation in parliament will be to no avail: we will simply replace some members of the old guard with others. On the contrary, the key is to ensure that society embraces politics. In order for the parties to be revitalized, they need to rediscover their *raison d'être*: to educate, to deliberate, and to make proposals. Educate and ensure that new talent can be nurtured—for example, by supporting young people who want to learn public speaking and get into politics.

The movement that we have launched, *En Marche!*, must provide an example for others in that regard. It is for this reason that I have been adamant that women and men from civil society should have access to positions of responsibility. They form the majority of our ranks; more than 60 per cent of our national delegates and local officers are not campaigning for election, and have never done so. Within this new movement, we will also ensure that responsibilities are conferred for limited periods.

This kind of improved representation is just as essential in the realm of the trade unions. We will only achieve strong trade union membership, which is essential, if we encourage it by allocating human resources based on employees' choices; if we give unions more real responsibility in industry bodies and at companies; and if the trade unions are capable of remodeling themselves. This means shaping careers where national representatives are not people who accumulate functions that remove them from workers' daily lives, but where, once again, commitment is taken into account, and responsibilities have a finite duration.

There must be no question of slipping into a rhetoric that stigmatizes elected, political, and union representatives. What is unacceptable is when a caste builds itself up, closes ranks, and imposes its own rules. And here the parties and institutions are far more to blame than the representatives themselves. Let us remember that when we talk about elected representatives, we are also talking about the 375,000 French people who work as volunteers on our 36,500 municipal councils. And we must not forget that union representatives do not ration either their time or their dedication.

Equally, the upper echelons of the civil service must not be exempt from meeting the highest standards. Although public officials may have formed a caste and give the impression that they are managing the country's affairs in the shadows, they were selected by competitive examinations and are not co-opted through connivance and collusion, as are many political-party executives. The highest-grade posts, and there are almost 300 of them, are appointed on Wednesdays during meetings of the Council of Ministers. In that regard, I am in favor of retaining the competitive entry system, as applies at the National School of Administration and other institutions—because it is a merit-based selection. Of course, there is certainly room to improve the curricula and the type of examinations, but that does not come under the remit of a presidential election.

On the other hand, we must modernize the upper ranks of the civil service in two ways. First, by opening up far more management positions to people who are not already civil servants. However, this is dependent upon the state being an employer capable of attracting talent—which is not currently the case. The state pays its workforce badly, and is often ungrateful. Political leaders use these appointments more often to support their cronies than to recruit people with exceptional profiles.

Next, it is no longer acceptable for high-ranking officials to enjoy everlasting protection. Belonging to a closed circle, having a right to take up one's post again at any time—these are protections that no longer correspond either to our era or to practices in wider society. When a person is one of those who manage affairs of state, it is logical that they should be protected, and it is also a guarantee of neutrality and independence. But this must go hand in hand with an element of risk in terms of job security and with stricter appraisals. Above all, protection must not be acquired for all time. Privileges must be attached to a position only, and not to an administrative body that protects its members for the rest of their lives.

It is for the above reasons, too, that I decided to resign from the civil service as I stood for the presidential election. Not that I believe that all civil servants should resign in order to be candidates. But I wanted to be consistent with the position on risk-taking and responsibility that I advocate for the rest of society.

Responsibility is precisely what, in my opinion, could restore some of our sorely needed collective morale.

Responsibility is first and foremost that of the government to the people, represented by parliament. The current system fosters a lack of responsibility, of which there are many instances. Regarding military intervention in Libya, for example, the British put in place a foreign-affairs committee to determine whether British leaders were right to initiate the Franco–British intervention, despite the geopolitical consequences that it led to. Did we do that, and if so, did we do it with sufficient diligence? Any event with a substantial impact on our national security should naturally give rise to the possibility of a parliamentary inquiry.

In parallel, ministers' responsibility must be cultivated. It is most important to have transparent checks on the probity and integrity of any person who is appointed as a minister. For this reason, appointment to ministerial office should be subject to the condition of a clean police record, as is already the case for the civil service. In fact, that is what we have put in practice for positions of responsibility at *En Marche!* The expertise and potential of a person appointed to participate in a hearing by a competent parliamentary committee should also be examined. What is more, when ministers are appointed, they must be capable of exercising authority over their departments, the people they meet, and the relevant business sectors.

The ultimate responsibility is a political one. Practices that are now out of place must be transformed. For example, even after being defeated or following democratic sanctions, no one leaves the political arena any more. Political responsibility also means playing by the rules and having the dignity to draw certain conclusions when one has lost one's way. Can a person seriously imagine that they can preside over the country's destiny, or even simply stand for election by the French people, when their personal probity has been called into question? I don't believe so.

However, on this point, we need to be explicit. We can all make mistakes in life; to err is human. We are all entitled to redeem ourselves for mistakes that we might have made in the past. That is just and fair. But when a person is a political leader, and when one is proposing to take the highest office in the land and represent our country, I believe that we need to make distinctions: not all mistakes are equal. Some of them—such as engaging in misconduct in public office, challenging state authority, or misappropriating political funds—ought to lead to outright disqualification from holding office. In such cases, people should have the decency to step aside. In any event, that is my own conception of political commitment and responsibility. Before asking people to entrust you with responsibilities, you first need to shoulder your own.

So why would we be more effective? Why should we succeed where so many others have failed?

First of all, I do not believe that failure is inevitable. If we want politics to serve the French people once again, we need to get down to the job of making politics more effective.

Today, French citizens have the impression that their government no longer governs. Whether in the matters of Europe, political parties, markets, opinion polls, or the street, there is confusion about who holds power. The government therefore needs to reclaim control, and explain what it is doing, because explanations enable society to accept what is being done. When governments fail to have a clear message, the people turn against them. Why were the 1995 reforms blocked by society? Because neither the then French president, in his manifesto, nor his prime minister, in exercising power, had taken the trouble to explain. Why did the Employment Act provoke so much indignation? For the same reason: because neither the president nor the prime minister of the time had taken pains to make matters clear.

It is important to be frank and open, and to explain, rather than to engage in PR campaigns. Today, governments tweet and issue press releases instead of providing explanations and taking a long-term approach. We must therefore create an environment conducive to clear communication by the government.

Furthermore, if we want to govern openly, we must not shy away from identifying matters that are beyond our control. Full transparency requires us to make it known when we do not have the means to take action.

Being effective means doing away with over-regulation: putting an end to overzealous transposition of European Union directives; putting an end to ad hoc legislation. The old French habit of creating rules or laws about every subject under the sun has become untenable. There have been more than fifty reforms of the labor market in fifteen years! During that time, unemployment has been rising continually—proof that laws are not the cure for all ills.

Before starting to draft a new rule, one must begin by carrying out a thorough assessment of the situation in question. More generally, by changing the structure, recruitment, and methods of the administration, we need to put an end to the belief, inherited from the nineteenth century, that considers drafting a law the be-all and end-all of official action. The goal needs to be the completion of a project, and not the enactment of a law. And this presupposes a sea change in the role of public stakeholders. Public policy is more effective when created hand in hand with the compatriots for whom it is intended. This applies to the fight against poverty, education policy, and many other areas.

In addition, laws must be tabled and debated more swiftly. It is urgent to reconcile the timeline for the democratic process and decision-making with lead times in real life and in the business world. I experienced this myself when the Growth, Economic Activity and Equal Economic Opportunity Act was discussed. I spent several hundred hours, first on a commission and then in session, debating the same subsections of the law with the same people—once, twice, three, and even four times! Currently, it takes over a year, on average, for a law to be passed, and at least as long, apart from a few exceptions, to pass the implementing decrees. Clearly, the process for adopting laws must be reviewed.

At the same time, we need to extend assessments of policies still in force, and step up oversight of government action. Impact assessment must become systematic. How many laws passed are, in fact, not implemented? And how many laws that are implemented fail to fulfill their initial goals? Every time a law is passed, it should thus be mandatory to assess its effectiveness two years after it enters into force. Each key text should have a repeal clause built in that will come into play in the absence of probative assessment.

Effectiveness also means guaranteeing the stability of legislation. We cannot during the same mandate change the structure of a tax or a public policy every year or every semester. The assessment process that I have just outlined provides a reasonable safety net, but is not sufficient. I want to ensure that a tax or a policy is only altered once during a five-year presidential term. That commitment is an indispensable component of effectiveness.

All of the above goes hand in hand, of course, with a complete reorganization of the way in which the state is run. Here, too, we need restraint and stability, with few ministers and stable perimeters. The law, regulations, and ministerial circulars need to define the framework, but autonomy in the field is now vital. At the state level, we must give power back to those who are best acquainted with realities, and place trust in our agents: in hospitals, schools, police stations, and prisons. We need to give them more autonomy, because they all have to deal with specific issues that cannot be resolved by a central state authority.

A new stage in what we might call 'de-convergence' is needed here. It means transferring power and responsibilities from the central administration to authorities on the ground and in direct contact with the general public. Those on the ground are aware of the solutions, and are often able to reach practical agreements with other stakeholders, whereas central directorates and ministries take more time, and are more inflexible and far removed from local realities.

Transforming the way in which the state level is organized means that we should examine the way in which the administration and civil servants are managed. We must create a more open and a more versatile system. Open, by facilitating diverse recruitment from the private sector, at all career stages, and to all grades of public service. Versatile, in order to best meet users' needs, so that civil servants are located where needs are most pronounced, and to offer them new career opportunities.

As we can see, the civil service as it currently stands no longer meets our citizens' expectations or the realities of the state, hospitals, or local authorities. This is not the civil servants' fault, and here I would like to underline their devotion and their sense of public service. Nonetheless, we must, on their behalf and that of the French people, face up to our present shortcomings.

I am conscious that this restructuring of the way in which the state is organized will run counter to embedded habits, but this revolution is essential in order to make us more effective and to allow civil servants' initiatives to be fully realized.

More broadly speaking, I believe in a new democratic apportionment of power. I believe that we can achieve success by placing our trust in those who get things done, and by giving them more power. This new approach to democratic power-sharing will give the means to take action to all those who are best placed to do so.

We need to found a Republic that places trust in the local level, in society, and its actors to carry out a true transformation. This implies a level of discipline to which we are not accustomed: giving more autonomy to those who are responsible for taking action; daring to experiment, seeing what works, whether something is worth implementing, what urgently needs to be withdrawn; looking at everything that society does better than the state, and entrusting it with the relevant responsibility.

The idea I have of democracy does not consist of passive citizens who delegate management of the nation to their political leaders. A healthy, modern democracy is composed of active citizens who play their part in transforming the country.

Of course, the state still has a central role to play. That role must even be strengthened in certain domains where the state needs to play a bigger part than it does currently. In order to carry out its duties, the state must have all the necessary resources at its disposal. In order to provide protection against the major risks of life, the state must now take certain matters back into its purview. In order to secure the proper functioning of our economy, it must remain the guarantor of public economic order.

Local authorities and their elected representatives must play a greater role. In the next few years, we need to decide on increasing momentum in the transfer of power to local authorities, in order for responsibilities and freedoms to be as close as possible to the field of action. This decentralization must be accompanied by a pragmatic attitude that has sometimes been absent in the past.

Social security insurance partners must be given increased responsibilities so as to be able to define working conditions for each industry sector and at company level. Associations must take a greater part, as they do already in areas such as healthcare, education, community action, inclusion, and so on.

From now on, citizens themselves must be considered more as stakeholders in public policies, rather than simply being on the receiving end. I want to define an area of responsibility for each person, but to empower those who get things done.

We have an incredible opportunity: French people do not want to be pawns. They want to get involved in their country. They are getting involved already, and they are doing so more and more. So we must be appreciative, and give them further support. Because they are our champions—today and every day.

They are our champions, because essential action is being carried out by many of their number: those who get involved in a compassionate, unselfish way, for the sake of others. Whether they are activists, whether they hold office, or whether they are volunteers for an NGO, many of our compatriots take time out of their family life and give up their evenings—such as the millions of French people who get involved in our non-profit associations, and the 200,000 firemen who volunteer to protect our civil security. A wish to serve permeates the nation, whether through companies, associations, NGOs, trade unions, or territorial authorities.

The power of the state must continue to support them and ensure that their energy bears fruit. It must assist them, be more flexible, and trust them. That commitment, throughout the land, is the last link in our chain of action. It is what holds our country together. It is what guarantees our unity, our cohesion. It is the condition of the effectiveness of our collective action on the ground. It is what makes solidarity, equality, and liberty more than mere words. French people have a passion for their country and for others—they want to serve rather than to be subjects. Let us give them the tools to do this.

I have a firm conviction that we can be daring in the future, and shape our destiny with our own hands. And to do this we need only to join hands once again. All of the pages of this book are, I hope, a demonstration of this. It was that very same conviction that led me to write it.

At the origin of this adventure are women and men who, more than anything else, want to shape progress. Who, like me, are convinced that to succeed we need to trust our compatriots and never lose sight of reality.

I love the unselfish simplicity of the many French people who have never been politically active, but who are deciding each day to join us in this unprecedented initiative. I also admire the facility with which women and men from all corners of society are making an outstanding success of transcending past rifts, coming together, and finding their place in a single mission.

They are reconnecting with the noblest essence of politics: transforming reality, taking effective action, and giving back power to those who get things done.

Afterword

Each of us is the product of our own history, the teachings of our instructors, the trust of our families, and the failures we have overcome. As I write, I remember those who helped me grow and develop, and gave me a taste for taking action and for service. I am fully aware of the debt I owe them, and the determination that is etched in my heart. Would those who supported me and who are no longer with us recognize our world? It has changed so much. Sometimes it troubles us.

Despite this, I am convinced that the twenty-first century we are entering is a century full of promise. This optimistic determination has been my guiding principle since the beginning, and has led me to serve my country.

The digital, environmental, technological, and industrial revolutions that are taking place are formidable. France must play its part. We must not allow the gap to widen between ourselves and the United States or, even more importantly, with China, the country-continent that demonstrates its power a little more each day.

We will only succeed on two conditions. That we revitalize Europe, our opportunity in a globalized world, and that we revive confidence in ourselves — by mustering the energy that we have lacked for so many years, but which I am convinced is still present in the French people.

In order to do that, each and every person in France must, once again, have their place.

To spearhead this combat, the responsibility of the president of the Republic is immense. I am fully conscious of that fact. The president is not only vested with powers to take action. The president also shoulders, less perceptibly, everything in the state that transcends politics: the values of our country, the continuity of its history and, discreetly, the vitality and dignity of public life.

I am ready.

Because I believe, more than anything, that we can succeed. Of course, one doesn't just wake up in the morning with that revelation. The decision to run for the highest office of the Republic is the fruit of deep-seated and intimate conviction, and a sense of history. As I have said in this book, I have led other lives. They have led me from the provinces to Paris, from corporate to public life. The responsibilities that I have held, as a minister, have allowed me to take full measure of the challenges of our times. All of these paths through my life have now converged.

I want my country to hold its head high, and in order to do this, to take up the reins of our thousand-year history: that incredible mission to emancipate people and society.

That grand design is a French one—to do everything possible to enable humanity to grow.

I cannot resign myself to seeing a France that is fearful and that only looks backwards, an extreme France that insults and excludes, a tired France that stagnates and just makes do.

I want a free France that is proud of what it is. Proud of its history, its culture, of its landscapes. Of its thousand springs that converge on our seas, of its mountains. Of its women and of its men who have undergone so many hardships and yet belong to no one.

I want a France that diffuses its culture and its values. A France that believes in opportunities, takes risks, dares to hope, never accepts unwarranted gains, nor wallows in cynicism. I want a France that is efficient, fair, and entrepreneurial, where every citizen chooses their life and makes a living from their work. A country that has reconciled all of its different facets and takes care of the weakest members of society, and places full trust in the French people.

You might say that these are just dreams. Yes, French citizens have indeed had more or less similar dreams in the past. They brought about the Revolution. Some of them had even had such dreams before that. And then we betrayed those dreams, through a laissez-faire attitude. Out of neglect. So, yes, they are dreams. They impose lofty ideals and high standards. They require commitment—our commitment. This is the democratic revolution that we must bring about in France, to reconcile freedom and progress. It is our vocation, and I know of none finer.

Notes

Chapter one: Who I am

7   *I spent entire days reading out loud to her: Molière and Racine, Georges Duhamel … as well as Mauriac:* Molière (1622–1673) was a playwright, actor, and director, and a genius of French theatrical comedy. Jean Racine (1639–1699) was a master of French classical tragedy. Georges Duhamel (1884–1966) was a medical doctor, founder of an artistic community, and author. François Mauriac (1885–1970) was a writer and winner of the 1952 Nobel Prize for literature.

7   *They expressed their care and concern:* The words are from the tragic love song "Avec le temps" by Léo Ferré—a classic that has been covered by many artists worldwide.

7   *But in that respect, too, I cannot think about the Republican school system today without remembering my family:* The "Republican school system" has been a hot topic since the nineteenth century. In France there is great tension concerning the extent to which religion should be a part of schooling. There is also a strong belief that school should be free of charge and accessible to all, and of equal quality for all.

8   *I learned from Colette:* Colette (1873–1954) was a novelist famed for her sensual and sensory descriptions. Jean Giono (1895–1970) was a Provençal novelist well known for his rich imagery of that region. André Gide (1869–1951) was a writer, humanist, and moralist, and the winner of the 1947

Nobel Prize for literature. Jean Cocteau (1889–1963) was a poet, artist, playwright, and surrealist filmmaker.

10   *It was not, however, a life of hardship:* Jean Giraudoux (1882–1944) was a diplomat and dramatist who was particularly active between the two world wars.

13   *The consuming ambition of Balzac's "young wolves":* This is a French way of describing arriviste young men. It probably originates in the novel *Eugène de Rastignac* by Honoré de Balzac, where an ambitious but poor nobleman climbs the social ladder by using his charm and wits.

13   *The doors of the* École normale supérieure *remained closed to me:* The *École normale supérieure* is one of France's elite higher-education institutions. It dates back to the French revolution and now has a tradition of training those who enter government and the upper echelons of academia. Paris Nanterre University was built in the 1960s, became prominent due to its central role in the 1968 student demonstrations, and is particularly well known for law and economics. Sciences Po is an elite political sciences institute founded in 1872 specifically to train future politicians.

14   *I was fortunate enough to make the acquaintance of the philosopher Paul Ricoeur:* Paul Ricoeur (1913–2005) was a prominent French philosopher and historian whose thinking related in particular to theories of interpretation, in areas such as language, psychology, politics, and religion.

14   *Olivier Mongin, François Dosse, Catherine Goldenstein, and Thérèse Duflot:* Olivier Mongin (1951–) is a writer, essayist, and publisher. François Dosse (1950–) is a historian and critic. Catherine Goldenstein (1958–) is a mathematician with an interest in the history of mathematics. Thérèse Duflot worked closely with Paul Ricoeur on his various publications.

15   *Along with a few others, who became and have remained faithful friends:* The *École nationale d'administration* (ENA) is an elite French institution founded to prepare students for work as high-ranking civil servants and roles in government.

16   *It was then that I met Henry Hermand:* Henry Hermand (1924–2016) was a physicist, member of the Resistance during the Second World War, and a major player in the French press. He was also a multimillionaire business leader

in the retail sector, and, unusually in that world, his politics were left wing.

16   *It was he who introduced me to Michel Rocard:* Michel Rocard (1930–2016) was a leading French socialist politician who was also very active on the European Union political scene.

17   *It was at this time that I became Deputy Rapporteur-General:* The Attali Commission was formed by President Nicolas Sarkozy in 2007 to make recommendations and proposals for the economy. It drafted two major written reports.

18   *Throughout these years, I maintained an interest in politics:* Founded in 1932, *Esprit* is an independent monthly journal with an intellectual bent that presents "ideas of the times". It provides analysis of politics, society, and culture, and from the outset has been interested not only in what happens in France but also across the globe.

21   *Our priority was to protect our long-weakened industrial sector:* PSA Peugeot-Citroën is a French automobile manufacturer that had been in financial difficulty for many years when the government took a partial stake in 2014, leading to a turnaround in its fortunes. Chantiers de l'Atlantique is one of the largest shipyards in the world, building naval, commercial, and passenger vessels, some of which are iconic. Volatile changes in shareholding and financial difficulties in recent decades led to its provisional nationalization in July 2017.

21   *After the Paris attacks in the autumn of 2015:* On 13 November 2015, France suffered concerted terrorist attacks in its capital. The national soccer stadium and the Bataclan concert venue came under fire, killing 130 people and affecting thousands through injury or trauma.

22   *As Malraux said, "Anti does not exist":* André Malraux (1901–1976) was a primarily self-taught writer, intellectual, art theorist, adventurer, and politician.

Chapter two: What I believe

31   *General de Gaulle, like Pierre Mendès France:* Both Charles de Gaulle (1890–1970) and Pierre Mendès France (1907–1982) were pragmatic statesmen who were active in the period immediately following the Second World War.

33   *However, every five years each camp wants to restate the importance of party discipline:* The influence of the National Front, a party on the extreme right, has been growing sharply over the last few decades, partly due to tensions over immigration and national security, and partly benefiting from a protest vote that expresses dissatisfaction with the mainstream political class as a whole.

34   *Since the trauma of 21 April 2002:* Most unexpectedly, on 21 April 2002, the then National Front leader, Jean-Marie Le Pen, succeeded in reaching the final round of the presidential election, resulting in a face-off against Jacques Chirac. France was profoundly shocked: until that time, the National Front had always been viewed as a marginal political party. The general feeling after the election was that the country's image and values had been seriously tarnished.

Chapter three: Who we are

36   *In its words:* The Edict of Villers-Cotterêts was passed by King Francis I of France in 1539 in the eponymous town. It called for the use of French in all legal acts and official matters, replacing Latin and regional languages such as Occitan or Picard.

36–7 *During the Classical Age:* The Classical Age refers to a period between the seventeenth and eighteenth centuries during which there was great interest in the classical artistic and literary traditions of Greece and Rome. The writings of Rabelais, who lived from 1483/4 until 1553, were highly influential, and he was famous for a bawdy and robust style.

38   *The world of* Arsène Lupin: Arsène Lupin is the main character in a series of novels about a gentleman thief by the writer Maurice Leblanc. *The Count of Monte Cristo* is a classic by Alexandre Dumas which tells of wrongful imprisonment and revenge. *Les Misérables* is a historical epic by Victor Hugo about social ills, which follows a number of characters over two decades and is set in the nineteenth century.

38   *André Breton, who loved Paris so much:* André Breton (1896–1966) was a leading surrealist, poet, and writer. In 1951, he purchased a property in the isolated and exceptionally

beautiful village of Saint-Cirq-Lapopie in the *département* of the Lot, and spent much time there until his death.

40   *It did this by affirming individual liberties and developing education under the Third Republic:* The Third Republic refers to the period of French government from 1870 to 1940. The Popular Front was a left-wing coalition that emerged as a result of fascism, and held power from 1936 to 1938. The Fourth Republic spans the period from 1944 to 1958, from the Liberation until war broke out in Algeria.

42   *It is also the massacres of the Vendée ... and special courts:* Between 1793 and 1796, during the French Revolution, civil war broke out in the Vendée area in the west of France between republicans and royalists. It was marked by wholesale slaughter. The often-derogatory term "special courts" is used in France to refer to courts used for mainly political or military ends, such as during the Inquisition, the Revolution, the Vichy Regime, or during the war in Algeria.

42   *A song as obviously familiar as* Le Chant du Départ: The *Chant du Départ* is a patriotic song written in 1794, just after the French Revolution. It was also used to rally French troops during the First World War.

43   *General Diego Brosset, a Companion of the Liberation:* The title "Companion of the Liberation" was bestowed on individuals who had distinguished themselves during the Second World War in liberating France from the Occupation.

44   *The spirit of the Encyclopedists:* The *Encyclopédie* dates from the Age of Enlightenment, and was a collaborative venture and colossal undertaking to catalogue arts and sciences led by Denis Diderot and Jean le Rond d'Alembert, first published between 1751 and 1777 in around thirty volumes comprising both text and illustrative plates.

Chapter four: The great transformation

48   *[T]he pipedreams of closed borders and a country of national workshops financed by miracles:* Following the 1848 revolution, the provisional government came up with the idea of "national workshops", to be financed by the state and intended to provide full employment.

Chapter five: The France that we want

57　*We have become accustomed to an outmoded system of national education … an inadequate and archaic territorial structure:* France is divided into *communes* (~municipalities), *départements* (~provinces), and regions. This structure is now criticized by many people as overcomplicated and no longer relevant.

60–1　*New talents — Palladio, Veronese, Giorgione — reinvented the city:* Andrea Palladio (1508–1580) was an architect who was very active during the Italian Renaissance and whose work was heavily influenced by Roman and Greek styles. Paolo Veronese (1528–1588) was a painter known for his large-scale mythological and religious work. Giorgione (1477/8–1510), although he died very young, has been credited with liberating the style of later artists such as Titian.

62　*Like France in 1945 at the time of the National Council of Resistance:* The *Conseil national de la Résistance* was an apolitical association that stood against the Vichy government and aimed to unify and coordinate the various Resistance groups during the Second World War, and from 1945 set out plans for immediate action.

63　*Today, we no longer have the "great projects" economy of the "Thirty Glorious Years":* The period from 1945 to 1975 saw prosperity and rebuilding after the Second World War, along with demographic changes: the baby boom, a higher standard of living, consumerism, and mass production.

Chapter six: Investing in our future

67　*That dream was the realm of the state in the days of Colbert:* Jean-Baptiste Colbert (1619–1683) was minister to Louis XIV, the Sun King. Highly influential, he was particularly renowned for his control of finances, and his patronage of the arts and sciences, as well as his work developing overseas trade. He put in place incentives to encourage the production in France of luxury goods such as mirrors and textiles, and shipbuilding.

76　*The CICE (Tax Credit for Competitiveness and Employment) and the Responsibility and Solidarity Pact:* The CICE aims to foster private companies' investments, and to encourage them to explore new markets, engage in research and innovation, and recruit employees: it reduces labor costs via substantial tax savings. The Responsibility and Solidarity Pact was announced by president Hollande in January 2014 and defined by prime minister Manuel Valls on 8 April 2014. It is a government policy to renew growth and employment in France: to accelerate job creation by businesses, and to increase the purchasing power of low-income households.

81   *[T]hese people wish for the return of the* Plan Calcul: The *Plan Calcul* was launched by president de Gaulle in 1966 to develop information technologies as a way to make up for ground that had been lost by France in the post-war era to other nations. A number of French firms and their subsidiaries were grouped into a single entity with the aim of strengthening the sector.

Chapter seven: Producing in France and saving the planet

84   *The most accomplished experts, however, such as Jean Jouzel, have made the matter very plain:* Jean Jouzel (1947–) is a world-renowned climatologist who has made notable contributions to scientific progress on global warming.

86   *[O]ur overseas territories:* France has 12 overseas territories with 2.6 million inhabitants. In many ways, they function as if they were mainland France, with similar official procedures, but suffer from a number of imbalances due to their location and/or local economic circumstances.

Chapter eight: Educating all our children

96   *[O]ur school system:* The *grandes écoles* are elite and prestigious French institutions where the country's prospective business, intellectual, and political leaders are trained. Entry is by highly selective and competitive procedures, and workloads are notoriously unforgiving and heavy. See above: *École nationale d'administration.*

99   *[K]indergartens situated in the priority educational zones:* Priority educational zones or *"zones d'éducation prioritaires"* were the brainchild of educational sociologists as a way to address social inequality in terms of access to knowledge

and training. They involved "positive discrimination" by stepping up action in areas where failure at school is higher.

Chapter ten: Doing more for those who have less

126 *[T]he "Active Solidarity Income" scheme:* The Active Solidarity Income or *revenu de solidarité active* guarantees a minimum benefit for those without any financial resources, subject to proof of eligibility. It is aimed at fostering a return to employment, and was first proposed in 2005, replacing other measures for low-income groups.

128 *[O]nly three of the 40 largest listed French companies that form the CAC40 are headed up by women:* CAC40 is the benchmark stock-market index for France, and takes its name from Cotation Assistée en Continu, the first pricing system used at the Paris Stock Exchange.

128 *This was widely reported by the women we encountered during a public consultation:* Prior to the French presidential election, *En Marche!* volunteers carried out an unprecedented door-to-door consultation of 100,000 members of the general public to better understand their problems and the changes they wanted and recommended. The results were then used to build an action plan for transformation.

136 *There will also be an immediate outcome in terms of governance:* These changes in unemployment benefits will have immediate consequences because the state will replace the benefit agencies. It will be financially significant as a result of the cap to be put on allowances, which are currently a proportion of the last salary. In other words, more people will be protected, but the higher benefits paid out to those who earned high salaries before becoming unemployed will be significantly reduced.

Chapter eleven: Reconciling France in all its guises

139 *France, like the rest of the world, is facing the effects of "metropolization":* "Metropolization" may be defined as the process by which cities grow as the population concentrates there, at the same time leading to sprawl from a city's center to its suburbs. In Europe, these changes in urban spaces are

seen as potential motors for the economy, whilst at the same time being of concern to many—first, on grounds of a potential rural–urban divide, and second, with regard to how such spaces can be interlinked across national borders.

151 *[I]t would be natural to create a relationship between regions and conurbations:* A law promulgated in 2015 reallocated powers to regional authorities, and reduced the number of regions from 22 to 13.

Chapter twelve: Caring for France

154 *Gilles Kepel, Olivier Roy, and a number of others have shed light on this situation:* Gilles Kepel and Olivier Roy are academic political scientists who specialize in Islamic studies, with sometimes differing points of view.

157 *[T]he attack at Saint-Étienne-du-Rouvray:* In 2016, two Muslim extremists stabbed and murdered Father Jacques Hamel, a priest at Saint Peter's church in Saint-Étienne-du-Rouvray near Rouen, also injuring a parishioner.

160 *It boils down to … combating all forms of "communitarianism":* Communitarianism is a somewhat complex doctrine that emphasizes the community and society over the individual, but may currently give rise to ghettoization or segregation—in certain cases, supporting fundamentalism.

160 *[W]e cannot perceive our role within the nation until we find our place in its history, its culture, its roots, and its illustrious figures:* Georges Danton (1759–1794) was a leading figure in the French Revolution. Léon Gambetta (1838–1882) was an influential politician and statesman. The Army of Year II refers to the revolutionary calendar and to an extensive conscription of soldiers from towns and villages all over France, provoking riots and widespread bloodshed. The Senegalese Tirailleurs were soldiers recruited in the then French colonies in Africa who joined infantry regiments, and distinguished themselves for their bravery on several occasions.

161 *The same emotion that surfaces at public meetings when I refer to Gide or Aragon. The emotion I felt when I heard Abd al Malik cite Camus:* André Gide (1869–1951) was a writer, humanist, and moralist. Louis Aragon (1897–1982) was a poet, novelist,

and journalist who formed part of the surrealist movement. Abd al Malik (1975–) is a rapper, composer, writer, and film director. Albert Camus (1913–1960) was a writer, philosopher, dramatist, and Nobel prizewinner.

Chapter thirteen: Protecting French citizens

168 *[T]o paraphrase the words of the 1789 Declaration of Human and Civic Rights:* In 1789, representatives of the French people formed a National Assembly that passed the Declaration of Human and Civic Rights. It contained 17 Articles, and set forth a human-rights charter for that time.

169 *We have no need to add extraordinary courts, internment camps, or who knows what kind of "presumption of nationality":* A "presumption of nationality" is a highly contested topic relating to how proof of a right to French nationality may be provided.

172 *Hence Operation Sentinel:* Operation Sentinel was a military operation launched in January 2015 and stepped up later that year, aimed at protecting key locations in France from terrorist attack.

174 *[C]ommunity policing, put in place by Lionel Jospin and Jean-Pierre Chevènement:* Lionel Jospin (1937–) and Jean-Pierre Chevènement (1939–) are leading French politicians of the Left.

175 *[T]he appalling attack at Viry-Châtillon:* In October 2016, police officers and their vehicles were attacked with Molotov cocktails in Viry-Châtillon by a group of young people. This gave rise to subsequent demonstrations by the police to demand, in particular, an increase in resources.

Chapter fourteen: Taking control of our destiny

181 *[A] special relationship with the African continent and the Middle East:* When referring to the Middle East, the French language currently uses two rather interchangeable terms: "Proche Orient" and "Moyen Orient", while the English term "Near East" has largely fallen into disuse.

194 *[T]he work carried out in 2013 by Hubert Védrine, Lionel Zinsou, Hakim El Karoui, Jean-Michel Severino, and Tidjane Thiam:* The

authors co-drafted a report for the Ministry of Economy and Finance, published in December 2013, entitled "A partnership for the future: 15 proposals for a new economic relationship between Africa and France" (*Un partenariat pour l'avenir : 15 propositions pour une nouvelle dynamique économique entre l'Afrique et la France*).

Chapter fifteen: A new Europe

204 *[T]he commission under Jacques Delors:* Jacques Delors (1925–) is a French politician and statesmen who served as the president of the European Commission from 1985 to 1995.

205 *For the French people, matters came to a head in 2005:* On 29 May 2005, a referendum was held in France on the treaty establishing a Constitution for Europe. It was rejected by a majority of voters.

214 *A European investment plan … much more powerful than the current "Juncker Plan", must be put in place as soon as possible:* The "Investment Plan for Europe", referred to as the Juncker Plan after European Commission president Jean-Claude Juncker, focuses on boosting European investments to create jobs and growth. Its operation is based on guarantees to encourage investors to take more risks.

215 *[T]he debt and deficit objectives included in the EU Stability and Growth Pact:* The European Union's Stability and Growth Pact is a set of rules designed to ensure that countries in the European Union pursue sound public finances and coordinate their fiscal policies.

217 *[T]he digital agenda:* The current digital agenda, which forms part of the Europe 2020 strategy, has the main objective of developing a digital single market in order to generate smart, sustainable, and inclusive growth in Europe.

218 *As Mario Monti and Sylvie Goulard had proposed:* Mario Monti and Sylvie Goulard are the co-authors of a book entitled *On democracy in Europe: looking ahead*, which combines the views of Monti, a former European commissioner, later a head of government and member of the European Council, with those of Goulard, a member of the European Parliament.

Chapter sixteen: Returning power to those who get things done

231   *Why were the 1995 reforms blocked by society?:* A series of reforms were proposed in France in 1995, relating to the civil service, pensions, and welfare. They led to general strikes, and affected transport, the postal service, telecommunications, education, and healthcare. The 2016 Employment Act, the so-called El Khomri Act, set out to modernize the French Labor Code. It was followed by further reforms, through decrees, in late August 2017.